Cloud SLA

Cloud SLA

The best practices of cloud service level agreements

Bart de Best
Pascal Huijbers

Edited by
Louis van Hemmen

Colophon

More information about this and other publications can be obtained from:
Leonon Media
(0)572 - 851 104

Common questions: info@leonon.nl
Sales questions: verkoop@leonon.nl
Manuscripts / Authors: redactie@leonon.nl

© 2018 Leonon Media

Cover design: Eric Coenders, IanusWeb, Nijmegen
Production: Printforce B.V., Alphen aan den Rijn

Title:	Cloud SLA
Sub title:	The best practices of cloud service level agreements
Date:	3 February 2018
Authors:	Bart de Best and Pascal Huijbers
Publisher:	Leonon Media
ISBN13:	978-94-92618-00-9
Edition:	First edition, first press 2018

TRADEMARK NOTICES
ASL® and BiSL® are registered trademarks of ASL BiSL Foundation.
DYA® and TMap NEXT® are registered trademarks of Sogeti Nederland B.V.
ITIL® and PRINCE2® are registered trademarks of Axelos Limited.

Table of Contents

VIII | Cloud Service Level Agreements

Figures

Tables

Appendices

💡 Tips

⚠️ Pitfalls

⛔ Don't

Introduction

In this book, Bart de Best and Pascal Huijbers take a look at the cloud SLA concept. This concept has specific implications for the structure of a service organisation and the agreements required for it. Especially the fact that cloud services are hard to get a grip on is a point of attention. The user no longer knows where his / her software runs and where the data is physically stored. However, the quality and the desired functionality should be guaranteed. But how to handle that exactly is a challenge. This book helps to identify the issues that a cloud SLA entails.

Terminologies such as BPaaS, SaaS, PaaS and IaaS are explained in order to clarify the various possibilities in cloud SLA area and to build a total service provisioning. In addition, controlling the risks involved in the cloud concept is an important issue. In particular, information security is important to explicitly address, this concerns the quality areas of, Confidentiality, Integrity and Accessibility (CIA). The entire contractual recording of the service provisioning is also extensively highlighted. In addition, the various aspects are accentuated to achieve balanced agreements that ensure the overall cloud SLA concept.

All in all, a complete, in-depth book, in which the authors work out the concept Cloud SLA in detail. An important reference book for anyone who is in contact with cloud SLAs comes, or will come.

Dr. Louis van Hemmen – BitAll b.v.

Preface

Increasingly, internal ICT services are being replaced by cloud ICT services. In the traditional ICT services, organizations themselves determined which components composes a service. Organizations were also responsible for determining the functionality and quality of these services. With the arrival of cloud services, there has been a strong change. The construction of cloud services is often only partially or even not known at all by the customer. In addition, the functionality and quality of a cloud service is often only to a limited extent adjustable by the customer.

This does not prevent organizations from changing their opinion and starting to use cloud services. The biggest increase occurs in the so-called 'commodities' area. These are highly standardized services, such as office automation services and infrastructure services. But it is also possible to outsource the services that are more intertwined with business processes such as Customer Relationship Management (CRM) services and financial services.

An important question when moving services to the cloud is what agreements should be made. Of course, functional and quality requirements must be determined as is the case with traditional ICT services. In the SLA book [Best 2013] this has been extensively discussed. The question for cloud SLA's is: What's so special about cloud services now and what does this mean for SLA content? This book provides an answer to that question by giving an overview of important risks. For any risk, the customer of a cloud service must determine if the risk applies or not. If applicable, then the customer must choose to control the risk or not. In this book, countermeasures are defined for the risks to be controlled. This book is therefore an important tool in setting up and managing a cloud SLA.

We hereby thank the following people for their inspiration and contribution to this book and the fine cooperation! My special gratitude goes to all the employees of Cybercom who reviewed this English version of the book and to Jane ten Have who did review the complete book in the first place.

- E. (Eric) Coenders — IanusWeb
- J.A.E. (Jane) ten Have — APG-AM
- J. (Jan-Willem) Hordijk — Cybercom
- Dr. L.J.G.T. (Louis) van Hemmen — BitAll b.v.
- F.J. (Fred) Ros RE RA — Auditdienst Rijk, Ministerie van Financiën
- Z. (Zdenek) Sedlak — Cybercom

We wish you good luck with creating SLAs for cloud services. If you have questions or comments, please do not hesitate to contact us. Much time has been spent to make this book as complete and consistent as possible. Should you find any shortcomings, we would appreciate it if you inform us, then these items can be processed in the next issue. No rights can be derived from any errors and / or shortcomings in this publication.

Bart de Best (bartb@dbmetrics.nl), Zoetermeer.
Pascal Huijbers (phuijbers@me.com), Zeewolde.

1 Introduction

Reading guideline:
The first paragraph of this chapter reflects the background of this book (1.1). Then, the objective (1.2) and the target group (1.3) are described. Paragraph 1.4 discusses the structure and content of the book by briefly indicating what is being discussed per chapter. This chapter ends with reading guidelines (1.5).

1.1 Background

The purpose of a SLA is to make agreements between customer and supplier about the ICT services to deliver in terms of functionality, quality, quantity and cost. This should take into account the constantly changing business needs supported by changing technologies [Niessen 1997].

A SLA is a product of the service level management process. There have already been many publications about service management and the service level management process inside. However, generally no suggestions are given for the creation of a SLA for cloud services. Therefore, the aim of this book is specifically at this aspect.

1.2 Objective

The primary objective of this book is to provide a toolbox to set up and maintain SLAs for cloud services. The book is also intended as a reference for anyone who uses cloud SLAs.

1.3 Target audience

This book is primarily focussed on service level managers of information management, application management and infrastructure management. They are in fact responsible for the entire life cycle of the SLA. Secondarily, this book focuses on the staff responsible for the organization of service management processes, such as service managers, process owners and process managers. Of course, this book is also suitable for those who as a customer want to agree on cloud SLAs.

An important target group that does may not be forgotten are the auditors. This book not only provides a check list for cloud SLAs but also designates a number of audit frameworks for them.

1.4 Structure

This book is made up of thirteen chapters, namely:
- Chapter 1 Introduction;
- Chapter 2 Cloud defined;
- Chapter 3 Cloud service broker;
- Chapter 4 Cloud contract aspects;
- Chapter 5 Cloud service documents;
- Chapter 6 Cloud service design;
- Chapter 7 Cloud risks;
- Chapter 8 Cloud SLAs;
- Chapter 9 Cloud governance;
- Chapter 10 Cloud SLA measurements;
- Chapter 11 Cloud changes and projects;
- Chapter 12 Cloud support and maintenance;
- Chapter 13 Cloud SLA Check list.

Chapter 1 Introduction
This chapter.

Chapter 2 Cloud defined
The term cloud is not defined unambiguously. This chapter provides a definition as a basis for the discussion of the cloud SLA.

Chapter 3 Cloud service broker
Many customers want to get more and more services in the cloud.
The merging of the cloud services and the management of the contracts is often outsourced to a cloud broker, also called cloud service broker. This chapter discusses the role that may be expected from this broker.

Chapter 4 Cloud contract aspects
Besides SLA agreements there are of course also contractual aspects to be considered. Before entering the cloud SLA, this chapter first explains the main contractual aspects.

Chapter 5 Cloud service documents
A SLA is the basis for the cloud service agreements. However, there are more documents that each have their own added value. This chapter describes these documents and the mutual relationship.

Chapter 6 Cloud service design
A service that is agreed upon is usually described in a service design. This chapter describes the attributes of a service design and indicates per attribute how to handle SLA in a cloud.

Chapter 7 Cloud risks
A cloud SLA differs on a number of aspects of a regular SLA. The only way to get these deviations clear is get an insight of the risks of the cloud services. The countermeasures of the risks form the basis of the cloud SLA.

Chapter 8 Cloud SLA
Based on the risks identified in Chapter 7, this chapter provides an explanation of the cloud SLA.

Chapter 9 Cloud governance
Controlling the cloud SLAs is different form the other regular SLAs. This chapter describes the most important areas of attention.

Chapter 10 Cloud SLA measurements
There are various ways to monitor SLAs. This chapter gives a brief description per monitor type and describes what constraints apply to monitoring the cloud services.

Chapter 11 Cloud changes and projects
There a significant difference between the maintenance and creation of cloud services and normal services. This chapter provides useful tips and tricks.

Chapter 12 Cloud support en maintenance
Agree upon the support and maintenance aspects in cloud SLA's service requires extra attention.

Chapter 13 Cloud SLA check list
This chapter provides a check list to check a cloud SLA for completeness.

Appendices
A list of literature references is included in Appendix A. The most important terms are listed in the glossary in Appendix B. The abbreviations are listed in Appendix C. Because many ITIL terms have been used in this book, Appendix D contains a complete list of important ITIL terms. The specific ITIL abbreviations are listed in Appendix E. Relevant websites can be found in Appendix F. An index of important terms is included in Appendix G.

1.5 Reading guidelines

Abbreviations
It has been strived to keep the abbreviations in this book limited. However, for the terms that are used regularly the abbreviations are used, to improve readability. In addition, common abbreviations that have been used, are fully written at first use. Appendix B and E provide the explanation of all the abbreviations used in the book.

References
This book consists of thirteen chapters. References to figures and tables are shown in the text with blue letters, including the chapter number.

Reading order
The chapters can be read separately. For a good understanding of how to compose and apply Cloud SLAs, it is important to read chapter two as a starting point.

Perspective
There are several interest groups to be recognized with a cloud SLA. Each interest group looks at the cloud SLA from its own perspective. The main interest groups are user organizations, service management organizations and cloud service providers. For readability, this book is written from the point of view of the internal service provider (information management, application management and infrastructure management), as these form the bridge between the user organization and cloud service providers.

Model selection
There are various best practice service management models on the market describing the service level management process, each from its own perspective. This book is based on ITIL version 2011.

Terms
The terms ICT service and ICT products are in this book defined as services and products, unless otherwise indicated. For the convenience of reading, the term "service" also means the delivery of products. Appendix B contains the specific terms used in this book. Annex C lists the abbreviations. Because this book uses many ITIL terms, Annex D gives an overview of these terms plus explanation. Annex F contains the ITIL abbreviations.

Definitions
Some definitions of terms are represented in blue frameworks. These terms are also included in the list of terms in Annex B.

Tips
T-01 In the book, a light bulb is placed on the left side of the text. This symbol indicates that the relevant paragraph contains an important tip. These icons have a unique number in the format: <T-00>.

Pitfalls
P-01 There are quite a few pitfalls that need to be avoided when designing and managing cloud SLAs. The warnings are marked with a warning sign. These icons have a unique number in the format: <P-00>.

Don't
D-01 In addition to recommendations, this book also contains a number of aspects that are not recommended. These icons have a unique number in the format: <D-00>.

2 Cloud defined

- Cloud services can be divided into four layers, namely Infrastructure as a Service (IaaS), Platform as a Service (PaaS), Software as a Service (SaaS) and Business Process as a Services (BPaaS).
- There are three categories of cloud services that can be identified private, public and hybrid. The extent to which SLA agreements can be made depends largely on this classification of cloud services.

Reading guideline:

This chapter starts with a definition of cloud services in section 2.1. Then section 2.2 lists the different patterns of cloud services. Cloud services are often also classified according to the use of the services: private, public and hybrid. Paragraph 2.3 describes the differences. This chapter ends with describing the cloud market.

2.1 Cloud definitions

As often with important concepts, cloud services also have no clear definition. Two commonly used definitions are those of Wikipedia and NIST as shown below. In this book, these are used as the basis.

> **Cloud Computing:**
> The cloud represents a network that forms a kind of computer cloud with all the computers connected to it, with the end user not knowing how much computer (s) is running or exactly what the software is. In this way, the user does not need to be the owner of the hardware and software used and is not responsible for the maintenance.
>
> The details of the information technology infrastructure are disguised and the user has an "own", scalable virtual infrastructure in terms of size and functionality. So, in fact, the cloud is a term that refers to online services [Wiki].

> **Cloud Computing:**
> Cloud computing is a model for enabling ubiquitous, convenient, on-demand network access to a shared pool of configurable computing resources (e.g. networks, servers, storage, applications, and services) that can be quickly provisioned and released with minimal management effort or service provider interaction [NIST].

When describing cloud as understanding concept, it is not just about the definition of cloud but also of the attributes that can be related to a cloud service. In other words, what makes something a cloud service? According to the definition, only a service (such as data storage) that uses shared resources can be seen as a cloud service. This is not correct and is a shortcoming to the actual cloud services. Here are some features of a cloud service that are applicable to a greater or lesser extent by "pure" cloud services.

Contractual / financial aspects
- directly online (web-based);
- start immediately without interaction with the cloud service provider;
- monthly cancellation (depending on contract duration);
- no start-up costs;
- no exit fees;
- pay online (in addition to any offline features);
- online billing;
- no fixed licenses for products to end users;

- periodic - monthly (possibly quarterly / annual) subscriptions;
- pay per user (registered, active or competitor);
- pay for functionality (in packages);
- optional costs for consumption (bandwidth, storage, funds);
- there is always a base of shared services for multiple users (infrastructure and platform).

Support aspects
- support via email, telephone and web;
- generic SLA with possibly "local variation";
- generic privacy and user conditions.

Application aspects
- applications and platforms can be used over the Internet;
- the functionality in the application is web-based;
- no / limited local software is required;
- multi-tenant setup, multiple tenants using the same cloud service;
- instant quick response (seconds);
- multi-platform and multi-browser support;
- no local dongles needed or hard hardware coupling;
- self-service capabilities for users (password reset, customize et cetera);
- the service is complete without the need for direct interaction with the cloud service provider.

Availability aspects
- high uptime, aiming for 100% uptime;
- scheduled maintenance included in planning;
- no downtime for backups;
- up & down scalable model (from several to thousands);
- full automation (for creating accounts, servers and services);
- automatic provisioning of systems;
- single management console;
- level of virtualization;
- service catalogue of services;
- relationship charging / payment with services;
- maximize load of the hardware.

If these criteria are not met then the question is whether it is a real cloud service. These criteria provide a sharper view of the positioning of cloud services.

2.2 Cloud patterns
In general, four patterns of outsourcing are used in relation to cloud, as outlined in Figure 2-1.

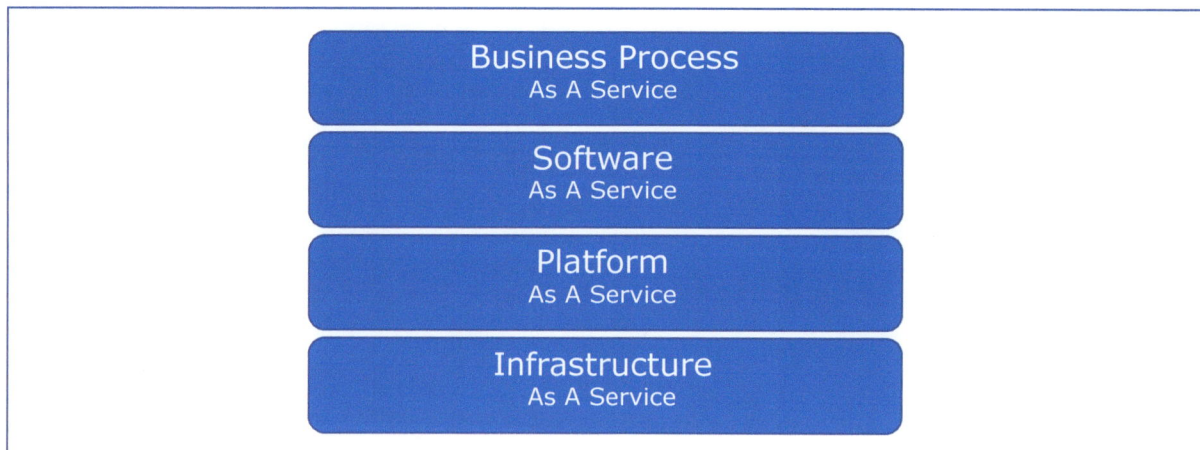

Figure 2-1, Cloud patterns.

The Business Process as a Service (BPaaS) concerns the outsourcing of a business process. The Software as a Service (SaaS) concerns the outsourcing of software functionality. The Platform as a Service (PaaS) concerns the outsourcing of platform functionality. The Infrastructure as a Service (IaaS) concerns outsourcing of infrastructure facilities. This book, where possible, uses definitions defined in the market. For the SaaS, PaaS and IaaS, the definitions of [Wiki] are used.

Business Process as a Service
BPaaS is a horizontal or vertical business process that is provided on the basis of the cloud service model. Either considering processes as functions that provide mutual services to each other. For example, performing a credit check as cloud service.

Software as a Service
In order to provide a SaaS service, the cloud service provider offers software "through the cloud". This software can be of all categories, such as email, customer management, personnel management, video applications, and so on. The cloud service provider has complete control over the software, but the customer or a third party who manages the customer can in many cases configure and functional manage the application. In many cases, the SaaS applications can be used via a web browser on a computer. Typically, modern technologies such as Ajax and HTML5 are used to obtain interactive functionality that is comparable or better than traditional client software. Many SaaS applications also work with mobile devices like smartphones and tablet computers. Also, sometimes a specific piece of client software is required and / or the application can be accessed through a technical interface (Application Programming Interface (API)) [Wiki].

Platform as a Service
The PaaS layer offers a number of services on top of the infrastructure that enables the SaaS providers to offer their applications in a structured and integrated manner. Examples of services in this layer are access management, identity management, portal functionality and integration facilities.

The customer of the PaaS services is a professional technical party that, in order to fulfil his role, must have the necessary degrees of freedom within the defined constraints

In this system, the framework and infrastructure are managed by the cloud service provider and can further control the software. There are often also facilities for development. This is often done with a development language or framework such as Python, .NET or Java in which you can define functionalities [Wiki].

Infrastructure as a Service
In this layer, you will find the servers, networks, storage capacity and other infrastructure. The infrastructure is presented through a virtualization or hardware integration. The IaaS allows the user complete freedom to the hardware. The cloud server can therefore be operated from an external location by multiple persons [Wiki].

At BPaaS, SaaS, PaaS and IaaS it is the outsourcing of services to an external cloud service provider. This provider provides this cloud service to various organizations.

BPaaS

BPaaS involves outsourcing complete business processes to a cloud service provider, consider payroll processing, mail processing, customer contact centre, debt collection of a manufacturing process. Usually, the reason for an organization to outsource a business process is to focus on its primary business processes. The outsourced processes have to be performed but have not the primary focus. Cloud service providers who supports this on a large scale have specialism and economies of scale and see this as a specialty that also gives them the availability of the right expertise, people and resources. Other reasons for using cloud services are flexibility and cost reduction.

It is difficult to stay well informed of all legislation, developments and opportunities in every area, just think of tax opportunities, financing opportunities, developments in sustainable service management and so on. It is not only difficult but also involves costs to maintain it even though it has not the primary focus. The client must also be in control and manage the process. The outsourcing of such a process ensures that the customer can outsource the performance of the process to an external party, and the client stays of course accountable. The customer is in charge and has to agree on the audit standard and quality criteria.

SaaS

With SaaS, the role of cloud service provider does not look much different. In this case, however, it is about providing functionality in the form of software that the customer can then buy as a service. An example of this is a customer contact system where the customer records his contacts with his customers. Instead of purchasing or developing a software product, the customer hires this service from a cloud service provider based on usage and the functionality that the customer receives. Characteristic of the cloud is that the customer pays per functional package per user over this period.

In general, the customer does not get this service on a private platform for himself, but uses a generic layer where all services for the different customers are executed. The cloud service provider is responsible for keeping this sub layer available and the customer himself has a number of options to configure his own functionality for his users. For many types of functionality, one or more cloud services are available somewhere in the world. Reasons for this are similar to outsourcing BPaaS, namely cost savings, flexibility and focus on core business. Starting and maintaining these services requires only direct and limited focus on the operation. Also in terms of costs there is a shift of investment costs to periodic operational costs. Services are easy to stop and start without complex ICT projects and without major investment risks. In addition, the customer takes note of the developments and innovations performed by cloud service providers.

PaaS

In case of the provisioning of a PaaS, the basic functionality offered by the cloud provider is used by the customer to integrate or develop his own products. This is not about developing applications, but about customized applications that utilize the functionality in the underlying platform. This allows the customer to easily develop applications that the organization needs and where no standard software is available, too costly or not fit for use. Platform functionality such as managing content or authenticating users can also considered as a service for the customer.

IaaS

Infrastructure as a service can be seen as "computing centre as a service". Instead of setting up an own computing centre or purchasing its own servers, the customer uses the cloud service provider's computing centre and systems. With current technical capabilities, the customer can also consider servers, databases or storage as generic services that he can hire based on the usage of the services This allows the customer to rent capacity and upgrade it as needed. However, the customer only pays for actual use or the reservation of the capacity.

2.3 Cloud classification

In addition to the format of BPaaS, SaaS, PaaS and IaaS, also a classification is used as private, hybrid and public, as shown in Figure 2-2. An important difference is made between running on premise systems or in common systems with a cloud service provider.

This makes a difference between "dedicated" systems or shared systems. In case of using cloud services with an external provider, this is the public cloud. Private cloud refers to the use of a cloud platform (shared) on premise or an isolated environment at the cloud service provider. In a hybrid situation, there is a mix.

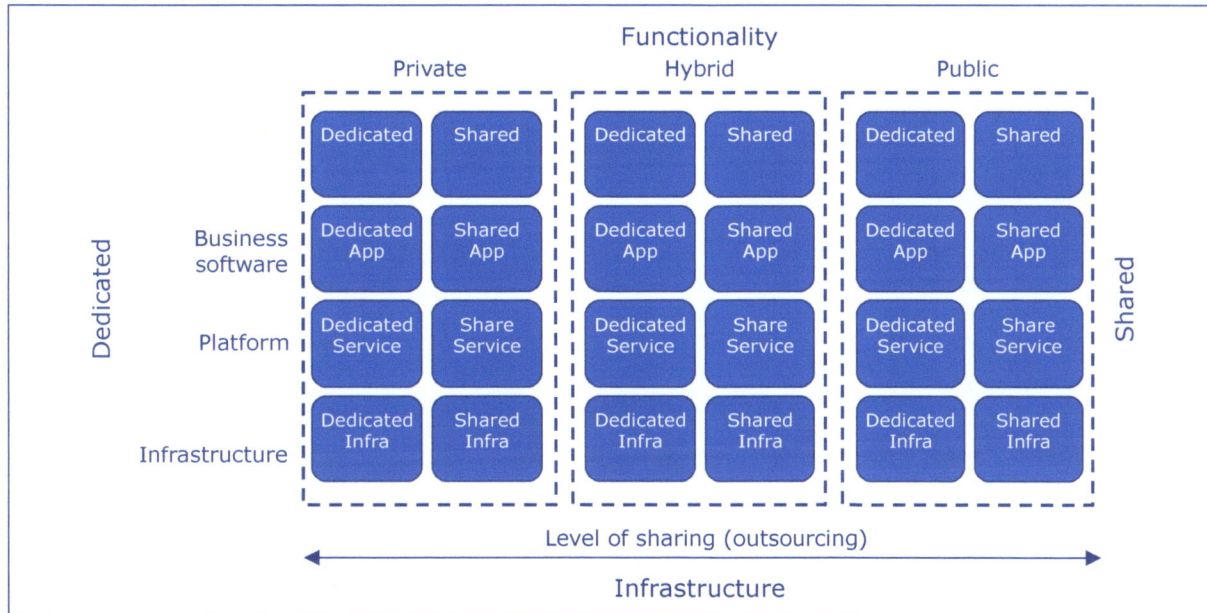

Figure 2-2, Cloud outsourcing, source: cloud sourcing levels – Clateway® (2013).

2.4 Cloud market

In Figure 2-3, the cloud market has been described using three patterns of cloud services, namely the SaaS, PaaS and IaaS pattern. The cloud market is wide and has many players.

Figure 2-3, Organisations in the cloud.

It is not just about cloud services and customers, but also the role of partners and consultants. In addition, new parties emerge such as cloud marketplaces, cloud service brokers and cloud aggregators. Traditionally, software vendors had to sell, advise, distribute, implement and support their software. Many different parties already played a role, such as resellers, distributors and consultancy companies, because they usually bundled software for their customers and advised them.

With the advent of the cloud services, it can be stated that customers can buy their services directly from the provider. The provider does not only provide software but also ensures that the service is available and can be bought by customers, including aspects such as management and support. Several major cloud service providers only know a direct model where the customer buys his service directly from the cloud service provider and pays it there too.

Distributors are no longer needed as resellers. Consultants only earn revenue by supporting selection and implementation. Thus, the cloud market is not only a technological change but also a change in the market model of the ICT suppliers. Figure 2-3 gives a first insight of the different levels on which the market can be viewed. This is certainly not complete and will need to develop further and stabilize in parallel with the cloud discussion.

Figure 2-3 also includes market segments such as the cloud marketplace, cloud service broker platforms, cloud management, cloud platform, virtualization management and hardware. Below is an explanation of the top three layers, namely: "Cloud Marketplace", "Cloud Broker Platform" and "Cloud Management".

Cloud Marketplace

A cloud marketplace is a place where providers, customers and partners meet. Cloud services are offered here and customers can compare these services to various aspects such as financial, contract, service levels, legal, management and engineering. Experience from other users is shared and customers have the opportunity to find a wide range of services and decide which the best solution is for them.

Cloud Broker Platform

A cloud service broker platform provides far-reaching integration of cloud services so that they can be offered to customers as a total package. For example, the possibility of composite invoices, payment in one currency, support of a first-aid helpdesk, one-time logon of services (Single Sign On (SSO)) and having a single contact for multiple services.

Cloud Management

Cloud management concerns the software and technologies designed to manage and monitor applications, data and services in the cloud. Cloud management tools help a company to ensure that IT resources placed in the cloud work optimally and interact with users and other services.

3 Cloud service broker

Message:
- Due to the increase in the complexity of the cloud services, there has been a need for a brokerage between customers and cloud service providers in the market. This is called the cloud service broker.
- The role of the cloud service broker is still strongly under development.

Reading guideline:
This chapter deals with a definition of the cloud service broker in section 3.1. Then section 3.2 shows the utility and necessity of a cloud service broker.

3.1 What is a cloud service broker?

In the first phase when cloud services appeared in the market, the customer was in charge. Thus, a SLA was needed between each customer and each cloud service provider, as depicted in Figure 3-1.

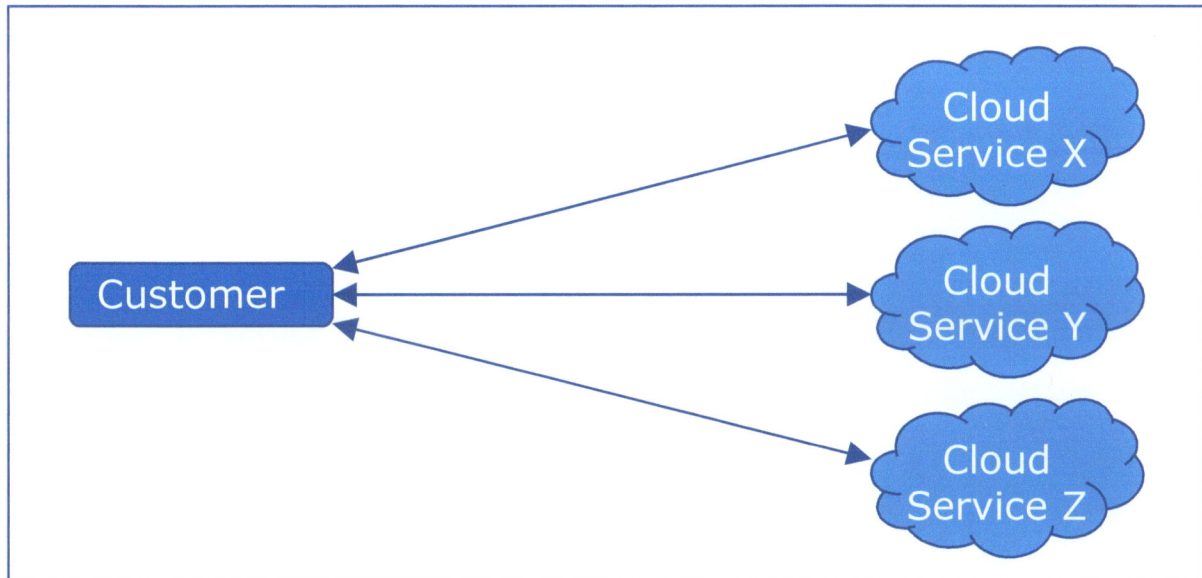

Figure 3-1, Cloud service model.

With the advent of increasingly different cloud services, many customers found the need for support in choosing the right solution and agreeing on cloud SLAs. This gap has been filled with the concept of Cloud Service Broker (CSB). Forbes gives the following definition of a CSB.

> **Cloud Service Broker:**
> A viable CSB provider can make it less expensive, easier, safer and more productive for companies to navigate, integrate, consume and extend cloud services, particularly when they span multiple, diverse cloud services providers [Forbes 2012].

A CSB is thus an intermediate party that connects customers and cloud service providers as depicted in Figure 3-2.

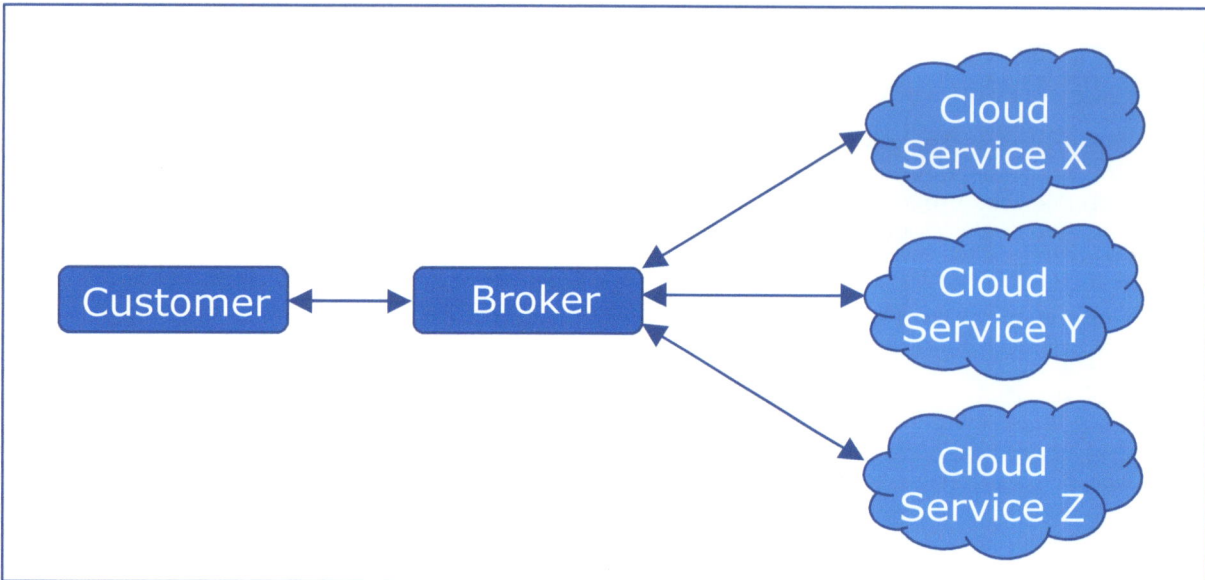

Figure 3-2, Broker cloud service model.

3.2 Why a CSB?

The CSB concept has become more important because of the further increase in cloud complexity, as described in the [FCW 2013] article.

> **CSB characteristic:**
> Brokers can take a complex situation for a consumer and make it simple [FCW 2013].

There are several arguments for using a cloud service broker. The main reasons why cloud service brokers can offer added value are:
- the CSB's opinion regarding the parties to be selected;
- simplifying complex situations for a customer;
- saving costs and providing information about the possibilities of cloud services;
- helping organizations to screen their applications for the use of cloud facilities and the corresponding prioritization of cloud migrations;
- helping to compare the various cloud patterns with variations in service offerings, including business models, service levels and applied packages;
- translating requirements to cloud service provider solutions so that an accurate estimate of cloud costs is possible;
- providing an opportunity to regulate international payments between different government agencies (such as currency conversions and payment mechanisms);
- providing an authentication and authorization integration feature;
- helping to create an agreement (contract / SLA).

Due to the growth of cloud service providers, an unambiguous information service interface, combined with a service, is a must for companies who spend their time implementing cloud services instead of investigating cloud services. However, the value of the CSB has not yet been determined and cloud computing is still in development. Perhaps the choice of a cloud solution becomes less complex. In that case, the CSB will have less added value.

4 Cloud contract aspects

Message:
- When concluding contracts, particular account must be taken of European privacy laws and the American Patriot Act.
- The role of Sarbanes Oxley (SOX) legislation is also significant.

Reading guideline:
This chapter deals with a brief description of the importance of European privacy legislation in section 4.1, followed by the US Patriot Act in section 4.2. This chapter ends with paragraph 4.3 in which Sarbanes Oxley's role is displayed.

4.1 European privacy legislation

European regulations formalize various requirements for data storage. It is the responsibility of companies to ensure that the data of that company contains (potentially) confidential information of employees and customers are stored in a secure manner. A company can be held liable for the leakage of confidential data and the company must then demonstrate that it has taken adequate measures to prevent that.

As long as a company stores data on its own infrastructure in its own data centre, it is quite easy to do this. But in case of using online cloud services the customer does not control the location and the way how data is stored, and thus depends on the cloud services provider.

In order to respond to European regulations, cloud service providers offer options to ensure that only storage facilities in an EU country are used [Wiki] [Info].

4.2 American Patriot Act

The Patriot Act is an American law aimed at combating terrorism. Under this legislation, the US government and government agencies have far-reaching powers, including forensic research. This implies, inter alia, that US organizations and companies are obliged to provide access to their infrastructure, such as servers and networks. Business units outside the U.S. territory should also cooperate in research. That means in concrete terms that US cloud providers cannot guarantee that data in, for example, Europe cannot be controlled by US government services. [Wiki] [ZDNET]. For this reason, it could be forbidden for European authorities to choose an American cloud service provider [Wiki] [Wedding 2011].

Figure 4-1, Signing of the USA PATRIOT Act by George W. Bush – Source: [Wiki].

4.3 Ten recommendations

The Branchevereniging Telecommunicatie Grootgebruikers (BTG) gives the following ten recommendations [BTG 2012]:

T-02

1. Try to understand and maintain the conditions under which justice and security services have access to data and the associated risks.
2. The possibility that data is being retrieved from the Netherlands by the American government, another foreign government, or Dutch government will be present to all cloud operators in the Netherlands. Approach this opportunity realistically.
3. Discuss the topic with cloud service providers. Aspects that may arise regarding the US include whether the provider is under US jurisdiction or parts of the service are outsourced to third parties (for example, to make backups), how to delete data in the cloud is organized and what happens to the cloud-processed data in case of bankruptcy, acquisition of the cloud service provider or upon termination of the agreement.
4. If, for reasons of the absence of US (or other foreign) jurisdiction, a specific cloud provider is chosen, it is recommended to include a specific contractual restriction regarding a takeover that could change the jurisdiction.

T-03

5. Make a good risk analysis based on a categorization of the different types of data that could be the subject of the investigations. On the basis of such internal analysis within the knowledge company, choices can be motivated and discussed with the direct involved. For information and data for which the risk that they actually belong to an American security service without any transparency being considered to be too high, alternatives could be developed.
6. A well thought-out and legally designed national cloud for the education and research sector is expected to provide better safeguards against the risk of access to data by a foreign government in a disproportionate way.
7. Where there is no watertight legal safeguard against unwanted data processing from abroad, technical protection measures may provide some significant protection. For example, well-designed decentralized and fragmented storage can prevent any data from being retrieved at once. Use encryption of cloud data.

T-04

8. However, in order to deal with particularly sensitive data, within a cloud context, good instructions must be given to users, just as it should be in a more traditional ICT environment within the company. Differentiation to the nature of the data and the way in which data flows may be desirable to ensure proportionality and effectiveness.
9. Ensuring a realistic exit strategy is as relevant as guaranteeing a backup of data and guarantees regarding the actual removal of data.

T-05

10. Given that the discussed legal issue is outside the field of decision of the stakeholders in the sector, it is recommended that the sector develop a clear position towards politics.

Meanwhile, there has been a new development that threatens further the confidentiality of data. The operation of the Foreign Intelligence and Surveillance Amendments Act (FISAA) introduced in 2008 is being extended. Article 1881a of the FISAA has enabled the possibility of large-scale surveillance specifically aimed at data within the US jurisdiction of non-US citizens. The Fourth Amendment protects US citizens against the FISAA. More about this can be read in: [Computable].

4.4 Sarbanes-Oxley-legislation

P-02

Also, SOX legislation in America could be a problem for the implementation of cloud computing and SaaS services. There are specialized companies that can advise organizations of these potential hazards. As with all SaaS and cloud computing services, there are potential objections.

One should be well aware that outsourcing confidential data is not without risk. Various IT specialists and lawyers have published about the potential dangers of these services [Wiki] / [Data motion]. In relation to this, it should be noted that the outsourcing of the service in terms of security and risks also has advantages. Because the relevant data is not captured and managed within the organization, it reduces the risk of internal manipulation, hacking or abuse. This should be weighed against the risks of external storage.

5 Cloud service documents

Message:
- When contracting a cloud service, various documents are involved in which agreements are recorded.
- What documents are required depends on the cloud service model.

Reading guideline:
When contracting a cloud service, various documents are important. Paragraph 5.1 discusses these documents. The documents are described from the perspective of an internal service provider that provides services to an internal customer. The internal service provider buys these both internally and externally. The coherence between these documents is described in section 5.2. Section 5.3 describes the different SLA forms for cloud services. Because the use of the document differs per cloud service model, section 5.4 first gives an overview of the models and in section 5.5 per cloud service model an indication is given what the relevant documents are.

5.1 The documents

With traditional SLA's various documents can be distinguished. The same is valid for Cloud SLA's.
- Service Level Requirements (SLR);
- Service Level Agreement (SLA);
- Document Agreements and Procedures (DAP);
- Underpinning Contract (UC);
- Service Catalogue.

5.1.1 Service Level Requirements (SLR)

Purpose
The purpose of SLR is to capture the customer's demand in a structured way. Reporting is necessary in order to analyse the required service provision for realisation and feasibility.

Application
The description of customer requirements regarding the service provision is described in so-called External Spec Sheets (ESS). This ESS can be compared with a functional design for an information system, however now only in terms of a service. After using the ESS for the design, construction and delivery of the service, this document must be kept up to date throughout the lifecycle of the service.

These requirements of the customer should be matched by the possibilities offered by the cloud specification (ISS) of cloud service provider. The ESS and the ISS together form the SLR. Strangely enough, the ESS and ISS are not used in practice. However, in many organizations, other documents are used to capture the requirements of a cloud service business, such as in a functional design of an information system. Of course, the negotiated requirements are clearly stated in the SLA and the service catalogue.

A possible consequence of failing to use an ESS is that information is missed, such as:
- what did the customer ask for, but was not delivered?
- what is the context in which the service is provided in terms of business processes and business services?
- what is the expected use of the cloud service?
- what are user-recognizable performance units?
- what is the location where the cloud service is used?

This information is important for the service level manager, because the customer's (dis) satisfaction can be derived from the services provided. In addition, a fully filled in ESS can be used in evaluating the SLA to see what changes have occurred at the customer which have an impact on service.

5.1.2 Service Level Agreement (SLA)

Purpose
The purpose of a SLA is to capture measurable performance agreements on the cloud service provider's cloud service provisioning to have the ability to account for it.

Application
A SLA is used to create performance agreements for delivering cloud services, products, and support processes.

5.1.3 Document Agreement and Procedures (DAP)

Purpose
The purpose of a DAP is to describe the agreements needed to ensure the SLA norms.

Application
SLAs include agreements between the customer and the cloud service provider in terms of norms regarding the delivery of cloud services, products and performance of support processes. To ensure that these norms are met, additional arrangements must be made. For example, the manner in which a change can be requested.

The reason for not including these agreements and procedures in the SLA is based on the size of the DAP and its maintenance. The DAP contains the description of procedures and it soon leads to thick documents. In order to keep the SLA clear, it is better to divide these documents. Furthermore, the maintenance of the DAP has a higher frequency. By dividing the contents into these two documents, they can be maintained and approved separately.

5.1.4 Underpinning Contract (UC)

Purpose
The purpose of an underpinning contract is to clarify the legal aspects of the cloud service provisioning to be agreed.

Application
The legal aspects of the cloud service may or may not be included in the SLA. In case there is a document that contains legal agreements, this is usually referred to as a contract. This is to emphasize on the legal aspects. Some cloud service providers find that to sound too harsh and keep the term SLA. It is important not to confuse a contract with an underpinning contract. A contract is a document between a customer and an external cloud service provider. An underpinning contract is an agreement between an internal provider and an external provider. In terms of legal aspects, however, these two documents are equivalent.

5.1.5 Service catalogue

Purpose
The purpose of the service catalogue is to unambiguously describe the services offered and to disclose to the potential customers.

Application
A cloud service is usually purchased by more than one customer. If each SLA includes the complete cloud service description, an unmanageable document will be created. Separating the cloud service description from the SLA eliminates or limits this risk. Often, in addition to cloud services, products are included in the service catalogue. Therefore, the service catalogue is also called the product and service catalogue.

5.2 The coherence

Figure 5-1 shows the coherence of the most important service level management documents. The user organizations' SLR is presented as the business requirements. These service support requirements are structured in the form of an ESS. The term "external" refers to the fact that the specifications of the services to be provided originates from the user organization (customer).

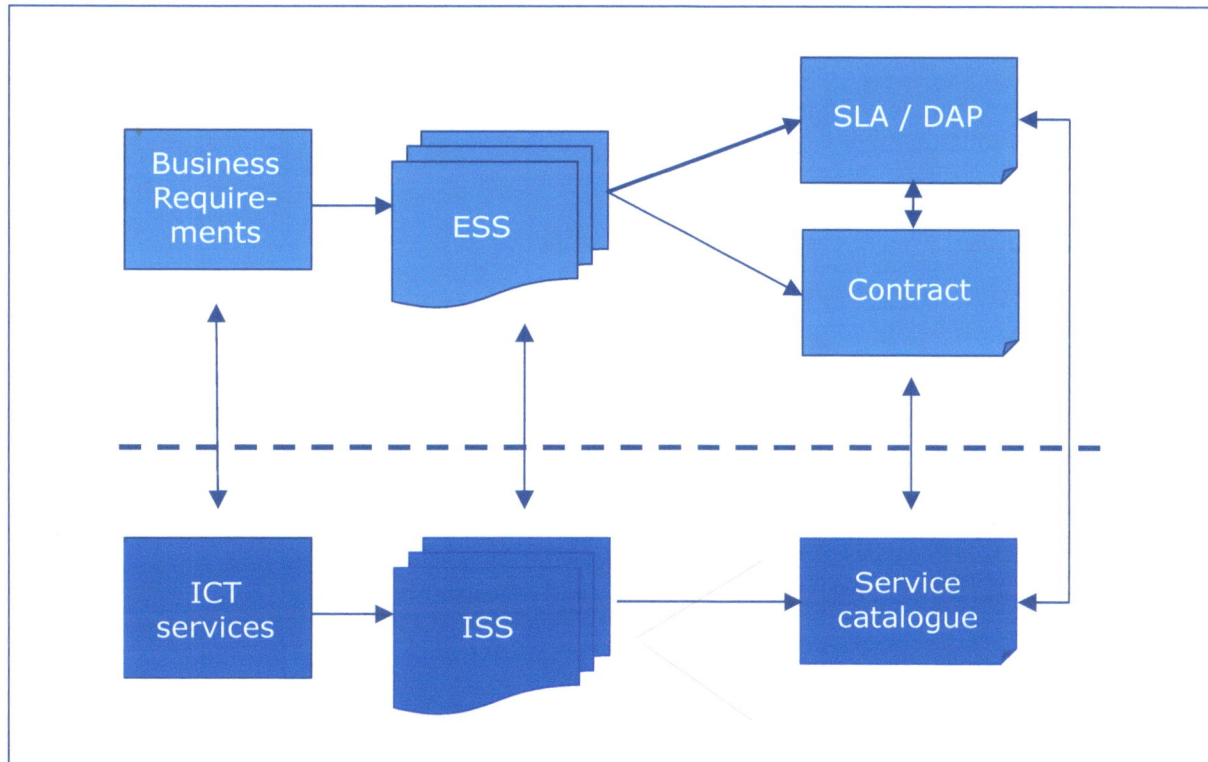

Figure 5-1, Service level management documents – source: [BEST 2009].

Based on the ESS, the service level manager makes an inventory of the extent to which customers' functionality and quality requirements can be met. The results are recorded in the ISS. These include the technical requirements that must be met in order to realize the services in accordance with the customer's functional and quality requirements.

The service level manager determines which services can be offered to the customers on the basis of the completed ESS and ISS. These services are included in the service catalogue. Possible additional services are added to this service catalogue that are not yet requested by the customers.

Based on the established ESS and service catalogue, the service level manager sets up an SLA. He also makes the arrangements with the internal and external providers to determine to what extent the delivery of the service can be ensured internally and externally by completing one or more Operational Level Agreements (OLAs) and Underpinning Contracts (UCs). Like a real estate agent, a service level manager cannot sell more than he buys.

⚠ P-03   The SLA agreements must therefore be covered for 100% by the agreements in the OLAs and / or UCs. After the negotiation with the user organization, service organization and cloud service providers, the service level manager will formally finalize the various documents by having them signed by a representative of the user organization and a representative of the service organization.

⚠ P-04   After determining the SLA, the ESS should not be discarded. They must be saved for the next SLA round. It may be that certain functional requirements or quality criteria are now unrealizable, but possible in the future. In addition to the above-mentioned documents, a number of other documents are used in practice. For example, a document is drawn up with the procedures and agreements called a DAP. In addition, a Document Financial Agreements (DFA) is also used to include the financial agreements.

SLAs do not exist in isolation. Creating a SLA that meets the requirements of the customer and is ensured by internal and external agreements with providers requires a thoughtful approach.
The requirements of the user organization should be translated into products and services that the support organization can provide.

5.3 SLA types
For cloud SLAs, three different types can be distinguished:

SLA's and wrap license contracts
Often, cloud services are unilateral contracts where a service level manager cannot negotiate a SLA (e.g., Apple I-cloud) - take it or leave it.

SLA's and standard contracts
Try to buy the default cloud service provided by the cloud service provider whenever possible. This saves time and money, and a higher risk coverage is also achieved. This applies especially to the public IaaS and PaaS services. But be aware of the not controlled risks.

SLA's and customized contracts
Here, custom contracts are agreed upon with the cloud service provider, with a SLA attached. The following topics are important:
- Rights concerning the inspection of the risk control of the cloud service provider;
- Obligations related to the commitment of the cloud service provider to comply with laws and regulations such as the personal data protection act;
- Especially applicable to private cloud and certain public SaaS solutions.

5.4 Cloud service models
There are several options for buying a cloud service. This book distinguishes four cloud service models, namely:
- Private cloud service model;
- Public cloud service model;
- Hybrid cloud service model;
- Broker service model.

5.4.1 Private cloud service model
Figure 5-2 shows the private cloud service model. In the event of a private cloud service, the service is based on an environment exclusively designed for the customer who buys private service.

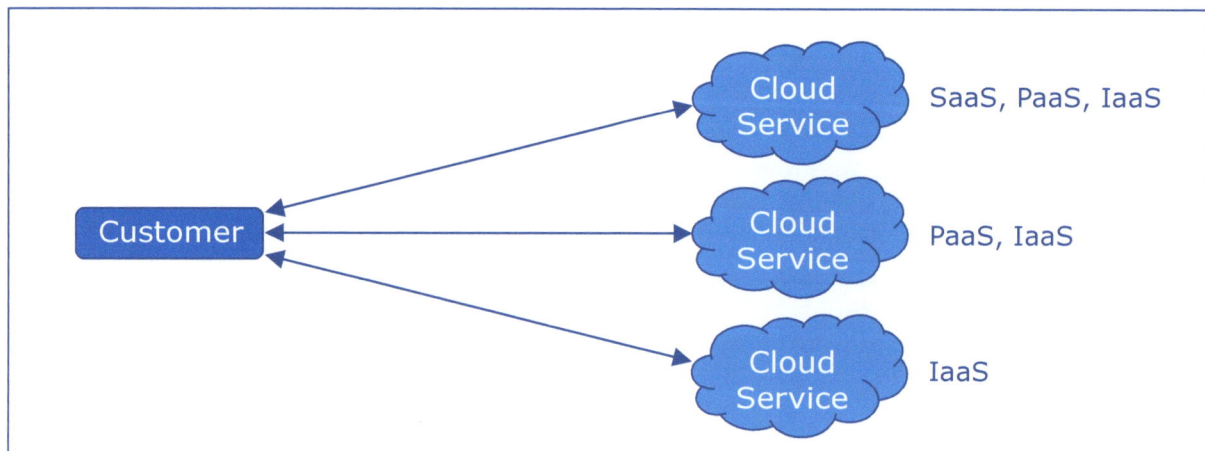

Figure 5-2, Private cloud service model.

Therefore, if the customer buys a SaaS service for a financial software package, then that software package will only be installed, configured and managed for that single customer by the cloud service provider. This in contrast to a public service where all customers use the same software package.

5.4.2 Public cloud service model

Figure 5-3 shows the public cloud service model. The cloud service provider delivers the services to various customers using the same facilities.

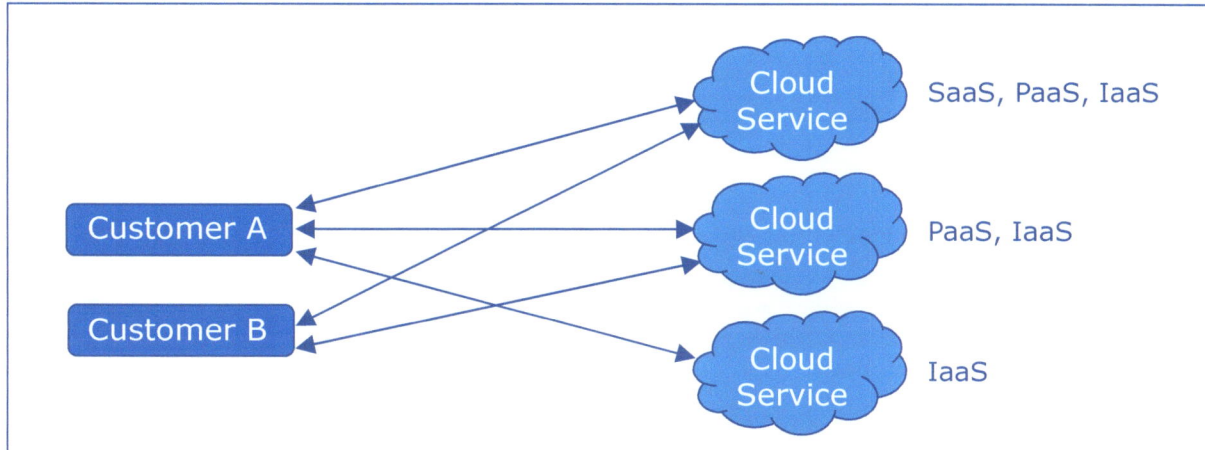

Figure 5-3, Public cloud service model.

5.4.3 Hybrid cloud service model

Figure 5-4 shows the hybrid service model. The service provisioning to the customer is based on a combination of services provided by the own support organization and purchased in the cloud.

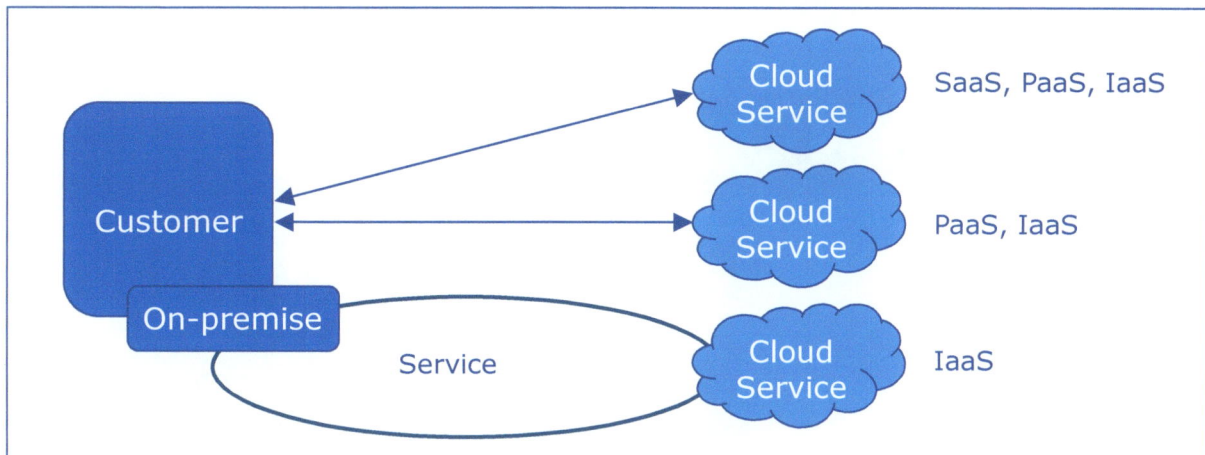

Figure 5-4, Hybrid cloud service model.

5.4.4 Broker cloud service model

Figure 5-5 shows the fourth cloud service model. In this model, the cloud service is bought from an intermediate party.

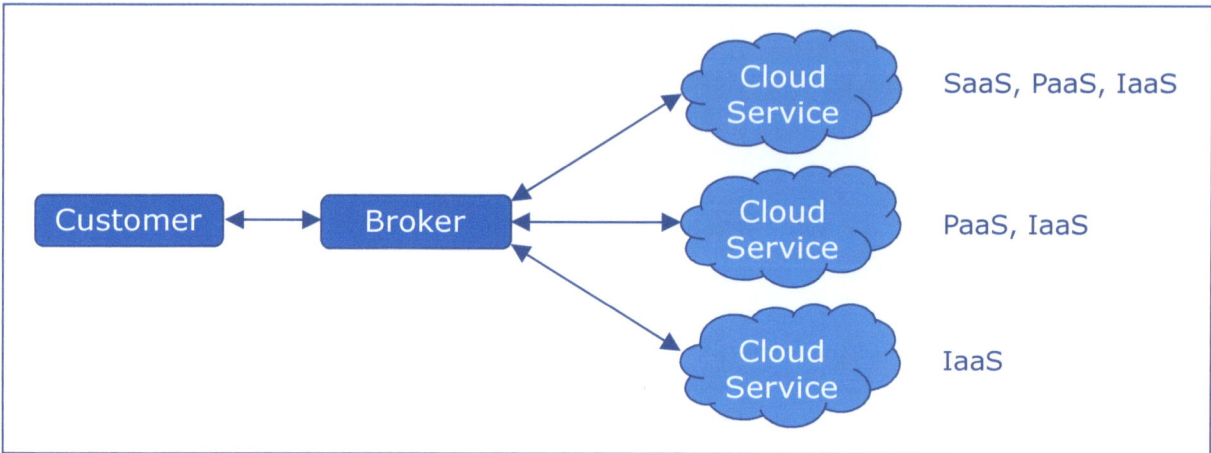

Figure 5-5, Broker cloud service model.

5.5 Documents per cloud service model

This section discusses the relevant service level management documents for the following four cloud service models:

- private cloud service model;
- public cloud service model;
- hybrid cloud service model;
- broker service model.

5.5.1 Private cloud service model

Figure 5-6 shows the service level management documents that are involved in a private cloud service. It concerns the SLA, which is based on the services provided by the cloud service provider. These services are included in the cloud service provider's service catalogue. The agreements are recorded in a DAP. The contract is based on this SLA.

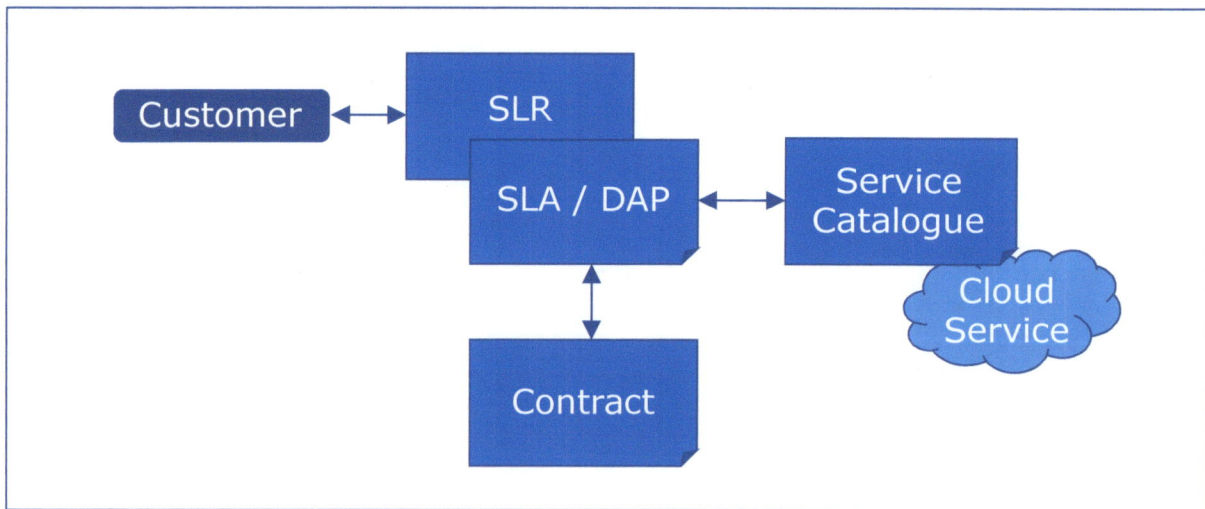

Figure 5-6, Private cloud service model documents.

The SLA and DAP are compiled based on customer service requirements that are defined in the SLR. The SLR incorporates customer service requirements in the form of an ESS. The possibilities that the cloud service broker sees to fulfil in these requirements are defined in the ISS. The delta between the ESS and ISS can be negotiated because this is a private cloud environment in which specific adjustments can be made for the customer.

In general, the customer can have great influence on the content of the SLA and DAP because the environment is specifically designed for the customer. The customer therefore has the exclusive right to use the environment. For many organizations, a private SaaS solution is an excellent step towards a public SaaS solution. The difference between an on-premise solution and a private cloud solution is not big.

5.5.2 Public cloud service model

Figure 5-7 shows the service level management document associated with public cloud services. The big difference with private cloud services is that the cloud service provider uses standard contracts that are equal for all customers. Because of the public service, these are standardized. The service catalogue is often published on the Internet. The composition of the SLA often takes place on the basis of a selection from the offered online services. Unlike regular SLAs and private cloud solutions, SLAs for public services are often much more dynamic, they are customized online, which also makes costs variable. This is particularly true for the IaaS and PaaS services and, to a smaller extent, for SaaS services.

Figure 5-7 shows the SLA and DAP and behind also the SLR document in which the customer has included his service requirements (ESS). However, in the case of public cloud services, there will usually not be an ISS in which the cloud service provider translates the customer service requirements in technical terms. However, the cloud service provider will indicate in its online service catalogue what services it offers and how they are composed. The customer can then test to what extent the Cloud service offering matches his cloud service requirements.

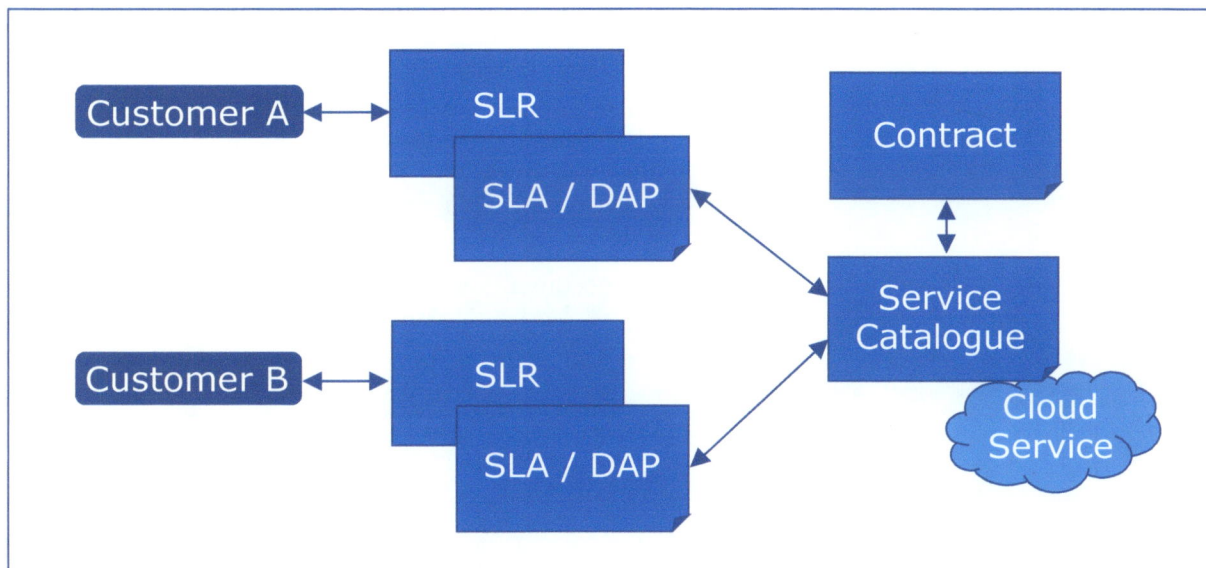

Figure 5-7, Public cloud service model documents.

Modifications of public services based on SLR are limited in scope because of the sharing of a common solution in the cloud. This implies, of course, that for public cloud services, the business process is often adapted to the SaaS solution rather than negotiating with the cloud service provider to adjust the service provisioning, if at all possible.

5.5.3 Hybrid cloud services

Figure 5-8 shows the service level management documents of the hybrid cloud services. The hybrid cloud services are a combination of public cloud services and traditional services. The internal provider can include the cloud services in the internal service catalogue, or can combine the cloud services with their own services and so offer them an integrated service. For example, an internal service provider can take a PaaS to install, configure, and manage a financial software package. A SaaS can also be purchased as a logistics software package that is linked to an internal service such as a financial system.

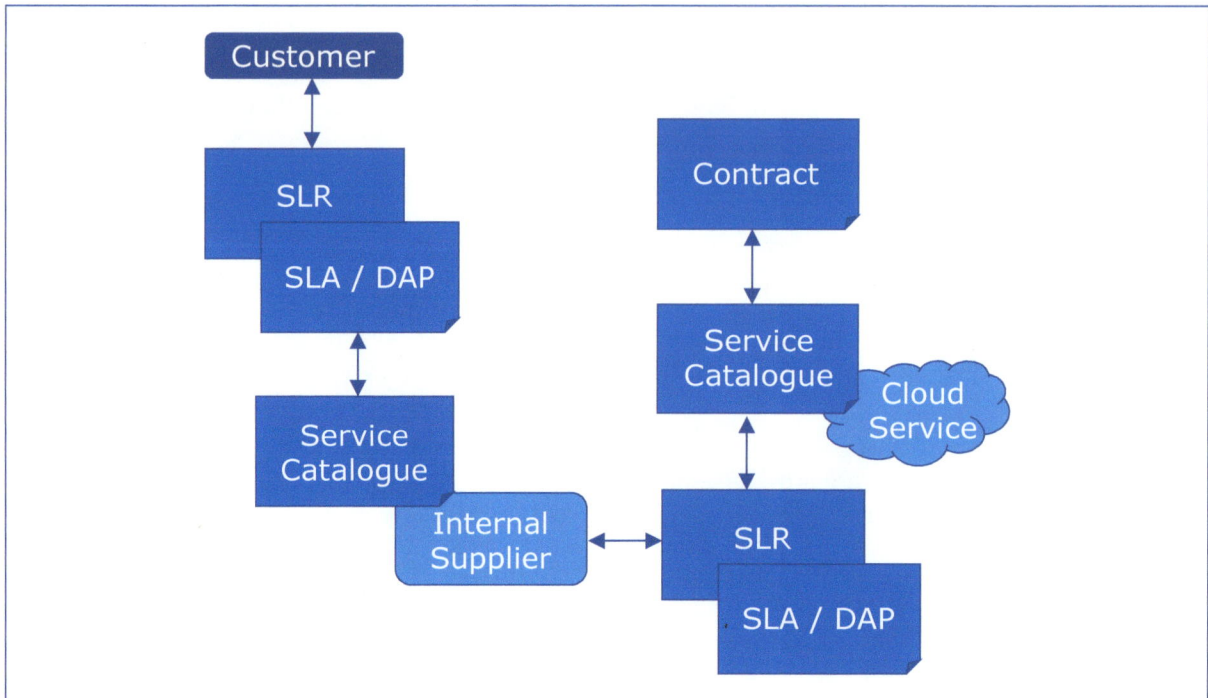

Figure 5-8,Hybrid cloud service model documents.

The total solution can be completely transparent to the customer. With this solution, the SLR document also has been signed between both the internal provider and the cloud service provider, but as with the public cloud service model, this will not play a major role in the private cloud service model.

5.5.4 Broker cloud service model

Figure 5-9 shows the service level management documents involved in case of a broker of cloud services.

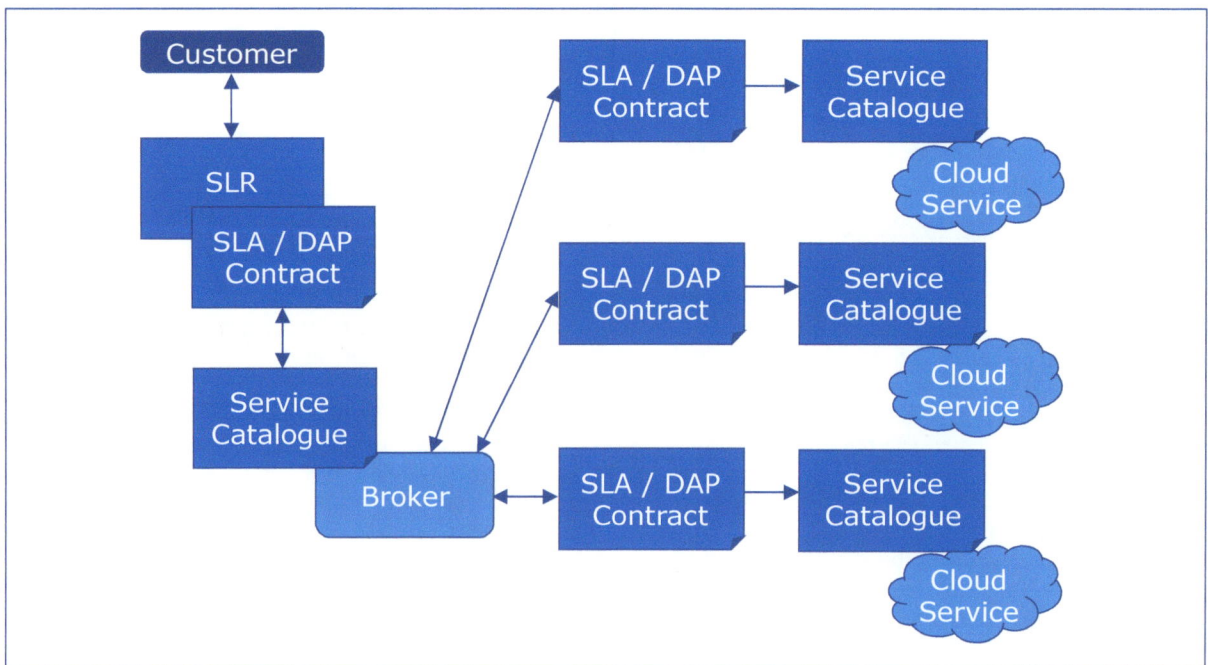

Figure 5-9, Broker cloud service model documents.

In case of a public cloud service provider, the customer directly deals with an external party. In this case the customer deals through a broker. For the sake of clarity in the picture, the documents SLA, DAP and contract have been merged into one icon. In case of a broker, the customer will also use an SLR (ESS) document to enable the cloud service broker to select the correct cloud services.

6 Cloud service design

Message:
- In the case of cloud services, there is often little insight on the service design. However, it is important to pay attention to the completion of the service attributes. Three types of service attributes can be identified: the general service attributes, the service utility (functionality) attributes, and the service warranty (quality) attributes. These service attributes form the basis for the content of the SLA.
- In particular, service quality is an important aspect, the customer has to compose a SLR document and investigate to what extent the cloud service provider fulfils the service requirements.
- For service quality, various quality models can be used to get own services clearly defined.
- The degrees of freedom to adjust cloud services are often limited. The SLRs serve to select a cloud solution rather than to adjust them.

Reading guideline:
The introduction (6.1) describes the general service attributes. Each attribute indicates which aspects of the cloud service provider can be expected. Section 6.2 shows the attributes of the service functionality (utility) and section 6.3 quality service attributes (warranty). This chapter concludes with discussing cloud risk management.

6.1 Common service attributes

A service can be defined by a number of attributes. For each of these service attributes, consideration should be given if agreements have to be formulated. This section gives a brief description of the major general service attributes.

Service definition
A good service definition must be given in which the target, the target audience and the intended functionality are defined in a one-liner.

Service owner
The service owner determines the functionality and quality of service. For a cloud service, the organization providing the cloud service can be considered the owner. With a private cloud service, an internal service owner can be defined as the owner because the customer has a lot of influence on functionality and quality.

Service contact point
The customer must have a contact point. This can be a service coordinator or an account manager. In the case of a private cloud service where the customer itself has an influence on the functionality and quality of the service to be provided, there will be a much more direct relationship between the customer and the service organisation of the cloud service provider and the cloud service provider may assign a service coordinator.

Service subscribers
The customer must receive a periodic reporting on who has obtained the service. Certainly, for a service where an organization's employee is free to obtain a service from a cloud service provider, this is important. An example is a role-based access. As soon as an employee gets a particular role assigned by a manager, the employee obtains rights to the services assigned to the role.

Service ordering
As with a regular service, ordering a service must be arranged in a DAP. This applies, for example, to new connections or new products from the customer to be included in the service.

Service counters
The charging on the usage of a service must be realistic and clear. Mostly, the cloud service provider will not issue a fixed price, but will require a fee that is related to the purchased volume. For example, the number of transactions in payment transactions.

6.2 Service utility attributes

In addition to general service attributes, there are also attributes that indicate the functionality of the service. In this book, these are defined as the service utility attributes. This section defines the main service utility attributes.

Service requirements

In many cases, a cloud SLA will have a limited possibility for defining functional requirements. Nevertheless, it is important for a customer to define these requirements just to know what is not being delivered.

Service components

The service components are the software and infrastructure products deployed by the cloud service provider in order to provide the cloud service. These are not visible to the customer and that is often not necessary. However, this poses a danger because it is assumed that the cloud service provider provides the functionality that is not explicitly agreed. For example, it may be very difficult to export or import certain data from the cloud service (interfaces) because the feature is missing or certain protocols are not possible. Also, data management may not be adequately supported, such as modifying data errors or changing business rules.

Law and Regulations (L&R)

The compliance of L&R must be tested by means of an audit. In cloud services, this is usually a Third-Party Audit (TPA) that the cloud service provider asks to be performed for all customers. Customers can then get a Third-Party Memorandum (TPM) describing to what extent the cloud service provider fulfils its obligations, such as, for example, an International Standard on Assurance Engagements (ISAE) 3402 audit. It is therefore important to determine which reviews the cloud service provider has executed.

Deliverables

The cloud service provider must clearly indicate which deliverables are provided and describe this output, in order to be able to provide a service. It is even better to make the cloud service provider accountable for his own service provisioning and the reporting on his performance or ask a broker to do this.

Preconditions

For some services, a number of preconditions must be met before the service can be granted. Agreements must be recorded in a DAP. For example, it can be agreed upon that the cloud service provider may only perform a year closure job after approval by the customer.

Activities in scope

In most cases, SLA activities are not visible to the customer. However, additional actions will be required when it comes to specific SaaS issues such as a quality control of the provided data. Who performs this review and what measures are taken in case of discrepancy is an important aspect of the agreement.

Related services and dependencies

The internal services of which service is dependent are not visible to the customer. The external are visible. An audit must indicate whether there are risks in the overall service hierarchy that the customer implicitly accepts. For example, for a SaaS service, the cloud service provider may have a PaaS contract with a party that does in not completely in control.

6.3 Service warranty attributes

In addition to general functionality, quality of service must also be described using service attributes. In this book, this is referred to as the warranty service attributes. This section defines the most important warranty attributes.

Service norms

The customer must indicate which norms are required for the agreed services. The service norms mainly concern the quality in terms of availability, security, capacity, performance and continuity.

Often, these norms will already be established by the cloud service provider and cannot be much changed. With a private cloud service this is of course a very different story. It is important, therefore, to determine to what extent the proposed SLA norms provide the control of the risks that the customer wants to cover. If the customer considers the performance or data recovery time important and the cloud service provider only wants to meet an availability level, then the customer must accept the risk of performance degradation and a recovery time that is too long or perform an acceptance test. An acceptance test in the form of a performance stress test and / or restore test will not always be possible and is a snapshot.

User profiles

If the cloud service provider offers custom service norms, then the customer must indicate what the expected use is of the cloud service. To this end, the customer must indicate which user profiles are recognized for the cloud services to be bought. A user profile is a description of the type of users such as an online user or a controller. Each user profile must address specific quality requirements such as opening hours and number of users. In addition, it is important to establish a relationship between the user profiles and business characteristics. To this end, patterns of business activities are recognized.

Patterns of Business Activities

T-06

Using the user profiles, the customer must also indicate the characteristics of the usage. For example, the administrator may only make online bookings during office hours, while the controller runs heavy reports every month.

The cloud service provider must determine on the basis of this data whether the quality and quantity requirements of the services can be met. A broker can advise on the right combination of cloud providers in terms of user profiles and patterns or business activities.

6.3.1 Service warranty availability

The availability of a service concerns both the availability of the data, the service services (core services) as well as the facilities such as a service desk (enabling services). Availability must always be considered from three aspects:
- the percentage of availability;
- the maximum number of disturbances;
- the maximum number of hours of a disturbance.

In addition, it is important to have some insight into the risks of availability. For this purpose, an overview is given in Figure 6-1. The availability is usually defined in Mean Time Between System Incidents (MTBSI). This value indicates the average time between two incidents. Between two incidents, we recognize a time of availability and unavailability. The average availability between two disturbances is the Mean Time Between Failure (MTBF) and the average unavailability is Mean Time To Repair (MTTR).

The MTTR is divided into five phases. Each phase has a certain characteristic about which SLA agreements can be made. The first phase is the detection time. If the cloud service provider does not offer a monitoring service, then the customer may be the first and only one to perceive a disturbance. An SLA agreement about the detection time is therefore important. The response time is the time elapsed between the incident detection and the actual service by the provider to resolve the incident. The diagnosis time and repair time are respectively the analysis and application of the correction. The recovery time is the time elapsed after repairing the errors in order to allow the service to be released for use. This concerns the start-up of the services and the possible recovery of data. For an average SaaS service, a cloud service provider is willing to agree upon a MTBF / MTBSI at the most. A reaction time agreement though is often added.

The question is, what is the measurement of the availability is. If availability is only determined based on a reported incident, the actual availability will be much lower than the reported availability. Agreements an availability based on a third-party end-to-end availability can be an interim solution.

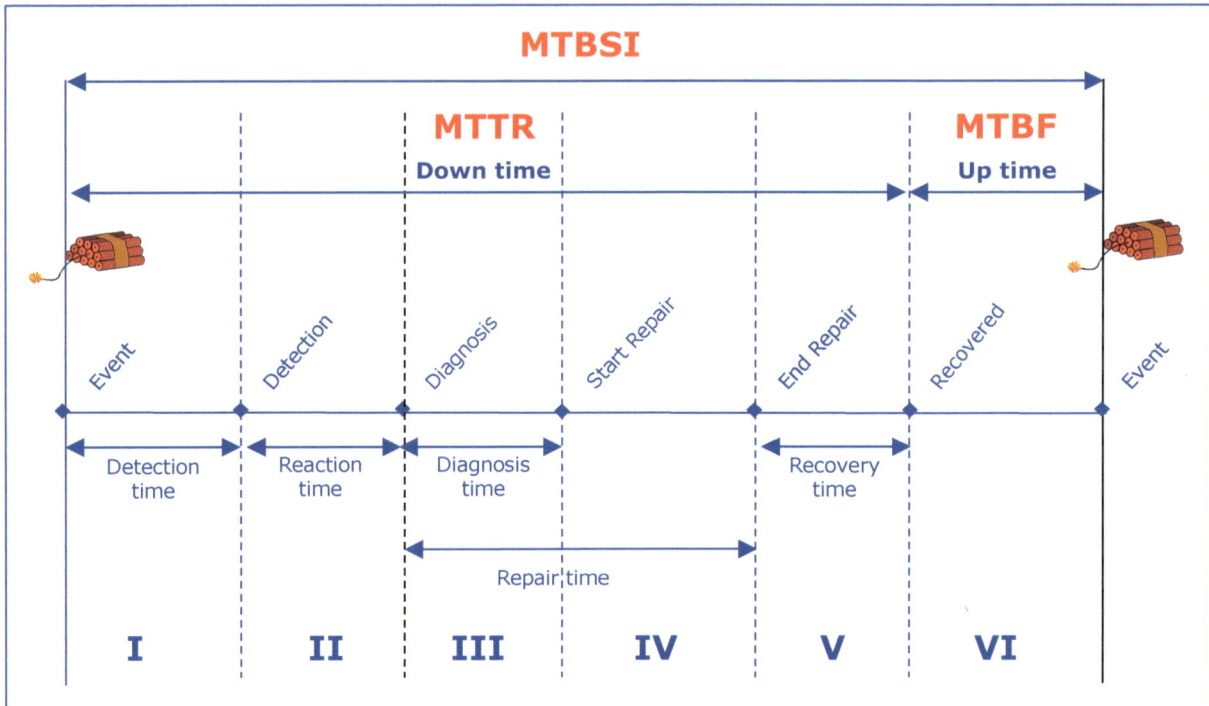

Figure 6-1, Phases of unavailability.

Key performance indicators for cloud SLAs are:
- detection time, response time, diagnosis time and repair time;
  - End-To-End (E2E) service availability;
  - detection time, for example up to 15 minutes;
  - response time, for example up to 1 hour;
- Mean Time To Repair (MTTR);
  - average downtime;
- Mean Time Between Failure (MTBF);
  - average uptime;
- Mean Time Between System Incidents (MTBSI);
  - average uptime + average downtime;
- reliability;
  - number of disturbances in a certain period of time;
- Restore Time Objective (RTO);
  - maximum recovery time;
- Restore Point Objective (RPO);
  - maximum permissible data loss.

It is important to recognize the relationship between the degree of encryption and the recovery time. The more encryption, the better the confidentiality is guaranteed, but also the more recovery time is needed.

The following monitor agreements can be considered:
- The norms are measured by a third party based on an E2E monitoring, for example by a cloud service broker;
- The cloud service provider itself performs a component monitoring;
- The cloud service provider is obliged to explain the non-compliance observed by a third party in the E2E measurement based on its own component measurements;
- The cloud service provider reports the availability in terms of service, priority, action and preventive action.

6.3.2 Service warranty continuity

The cloud service continuity can be controlled by both the cloud service provider as by the cloud service customer. The following measures are possible.

Internal cloud service provider measures

These are the options that apply to internal services:
- hot stand-by;
- warm stand-by;
- cold stand-by;
- fortification;
- redundancy;
- dormant contract;
- Definite Hardware Store (DHS);
- manual;
- do nothing.

These options are not further elaborated in this book, as it is adequately described in ITIL's best practices. The question is, what risks the cloud service provider sees, what he covers and how well the control is. In many cases, the cloud service provider will not make any statements about this. In that case, a TPA is a solution. The TPA must then analyse the continuity risks and the measures taken. The customer can get a TPM based on this TPA, indicating which risks are and which are not adequately controlled. An example of such a TPA is the control of a successful disaster recovery test.

Inter cloud service provider measures

A cloud service broker can provide continuity by connecting more cloud solutions. In case of an emergency, service is then continued by another cloud service. This is especially a good option for IaaS services. Important areas of attention are: data loss, compatibility and costs.

6.3.3 Service warranty performance

With cloud services, performance is an important quality aspect. The performance of a service is usually dependent on the following factors:
- the capacity of resources used such as the network, internal and external memory and processor capacity;
- the efficiency of software logic such as using the right indexes;
- the workload of the service such as the number of transactions, the number of concurrent users and the complexity of the queries.

In case of an IaaS and PaaS service, the capacity is custom-made and, of course, in the case of a private cloud service. In the event of a public SaaS service, performance is no longer adjustable unless the cloud service provider offers Quality of Service (QoS). This means that the SaaS takes into account the priority that a customer has when using a service shared by others. In that way, a cloud service provider can provide more service levels for a SaaS service. In practice, this is not often offered.

This means that the SLR document must explicitly determine the expected volume of services to be taken, such as the number of transactions per unit of time and the number of concurrent (simultaneous) users. These SLRs are then part of the selection criteria for acquiring a SaaS.

Important acceptance criteria for the performance of the SaaS service are:
- the cloud service provider guarantees the performance;
- performance is measured end-to-end and reported, preferably by a third party;
- performance issues are soluble by the scalability of the underlying IaaS and PaaS services.

A performance norms directive is an elapsed time of one to two, but at most three seconds for an online transaction. Heavy reports (queries) require more processing time. Therefore, it is important that the SaaS cloud service provider offers the possibility to make reports also batch wise.

6.3.4 Service warranty security

In addition to availability, continuity and performance, security is an important quality aspect of cloud services. SaaS service security must match the requirements as defined in the SLR. Security requirements are usually described on the basis of the Confidentiality, Integrity and Accessibility (CIA) of the information processed by the service. For each set of information, the CIA rating for these three aspects needs to be determined. In general, a classification of 0, 1, 2 and 3 is used for all three aspects, as described in Figure 6-2.

Security Requirement	No criteria Security is not really necessary	Advisable A certain degree of security is appreciated	Important Security is absolutely necessary in view of the interests	Essential Security is a primary criterion
Confidentiality	**Public** The information may be published / made public	**Protected** Data only to be seen by particular group	**Crucial** Data only accessible to those directly involved	**Mandatory** Business interests would be severely if accessed by un authorized parties
Integrity	**Passive** No extra integrity protection required	**Active** Business process tolerates some errors	**Detectable** A very small number of errors is permitted	**Essential** Business process demands error-free information
Availability	**Unnecessary** No guarantee required	**Necessary** Occasional downtime is acceptable	**Important** Hardly any downtime during opening times	**Essential** Only out of operation in extremely exceptional circumstances
	0	1	2	3

Figure 6-2, Security requirements.

Based on this matrix, the CIA encoding must be determined per service and registered in the SLR. After this it is necessary to indicate which security measures are required to fulfil this norm. The following step-by-step plan realizes this:
- Step 1. Define the information portfolio.
- Step 2. Select the information areas that logically coincide.
- Step 3. Determine which information areas are involved in the cloud service:
  - Create (data is created in the cloud service);
  - Read (data is used by the cloud service);
  - Update (data is being mutated by the cloud service);
  - Delete (data is being deleted by the cloud service).
- Step 4. Determine the CIA rating per information area.

Step 1. Information portfolio

The information portfolio comprises all the information that is used in an organization for all business processes. Within information management, management and maintenance of the information portfolio is also called information portfolio management, for example in the Business information Services Library (BiSL) model. The official involved in this process is often called an information architect or information analyst.

Step 2. Information areas

An information portfolio consists of a number of information areas. An information area consists of data clusters associated with financial data, customer data, personal data, logistics data, et cetera. Often, the CIA requirements of such an information area are of the same level.

So, services that are based on these information have the same CIA requirements. The BiSL process that embodies these activities is information lifecycle management. This process is also usually completed by an information architect or information analyst.

Step 3. Cloud services
The CIA norm per information area must be translated to the services that use the information areas.

Step 4. CIA rating
Per information service, the CIA rating must be determined. For example, confidentiality needs to be defined for each level. In practice, this means that requirements at level one are also applicable at level two and three, but will be heavier. For example, level one confidentiality requires, personalization of group-level information, while level two requires role access to information.

Figure 6-3, SABSA business attributes – source: [SABSA 2005].

At level three, however, access is required at the personal level and probably an audit trail has to be available on which is tracked who has requested, changed, or deleted information and when.

The CIA rating of an information service also depends on the usage of a cloud service. It is important to know per cloud service which data is Created, Read, Updated and Delete (CRUD). This CRUD analysis provides a good insight into which services require additional security measures.

In addition to the CIA rating, there are other models to determine the security level of a service. For example, the Sherwood Applied Business Security Architecture (SABSA) model has defined a list of attributes (business attributes) that add value to the business by controlling security risks. From this list of attributes, a selection is made based on the business needs of the business, such as the Balanced ScoreCard (BSC) targets. Figure 6-3 shows these SABSA business attributes.

6.3.5 Service warranty ISO 9126

A quality model that is widely used to define the quality of software is the extended International Standardization Organization (ISO) 9126 model. This is one of the standards published by the ISO.

This standard published in 1991 defines the quality of software based on a number of quality attributes. Originally, this standard only contained quality attributes: functionality, usability, reliability, efficiency, maintainability and portability. In practice, it turned out that this format was too general. Therefore, the set has been extended to twenty-one quality attributes. Later this set has grown to the Extended ISO 9126 and includes these thirty-two quality attributes as shown in Figure 6-4.

Figure 6-4, ISO 9126 quality attributes.

The quality attributes are considered as CSFs for service management processes. These CSFs can be made measurable by defining performance indicators. The dotted oval indicates whether the quality attributes relate to the business processes or service management processes. The quality requirements with regard to reliability and efficiency apply to both business processes and service management processes.

As common with classification models, the division into three groups (functional requirements, quality requirements and management requirements) contains borderline cases. For example, the Extended ISO 9126 model states that security and traceability are quality attributes that describe the functional quality of software.

In that perspective, these are quality attributes that can be a CSF for the business processes. For example, a virus checker may be a functional requirement of the user. However, the service organisation can define security and traceability in addition to functional quality, as well as service management quality. For example, updating the virus library timely is a quality claim from the administrator. Instead of security as a functional requirement, it could then be considered a reliability requirement. For this reason, the arrows and ovals are dotted. These ISO 9126 quality attributes can be seen as a check list for cloud SLA quality issues. Table 6-1 gives an overview the ISO 9126 quality attributes and possible synonyms.

ISO 9126 Quality Attribute	Synonymous
Functionality	
Suitability	Completeness
Accuracy	Correctness
Interoperability	
Compliance	Infinity
Security	
Traceability	
Usability	
Understand ability	
Learnability	
Operability	
Explicitness	
Customisability	
Attractivity	
Clarity	
Helpfulness	
User-friendliness	
Reliability	
Maturity	Reliability
Fault Tolerance	Resistance, Robustness
Recoverability	Resilience
Availability	
Degradability	Self-repairing ability
Efficiency	
Time behaviour	Response Rate, Speed batch processing
Resource behaviour	Resource usage
Maintainability	
Analysability	
Changeability	Correctibility
Stability	
Testability	
Manageability	
Reusability	

ISO 9126 Quality Attribute	Synonymous
Portability	
Adaptability	Portability
Installability	
Conformance	
Replaceability	

Table 6-1, ISO 9126 quality attributes and synonymous.

Functional quality attributes

Quality attribute		Description
Functional quality tells something about how the end user perceives the way of working with the software (usability) and about the logically correct operation (functionality) of the software product.		
Functionality	Suitability	The extent to which the software product provides the appropriate functionality for the identified tasks.
	Accuracy	The extent to which the software product provides the correct and agreed results.
	Interoperability	The degree to which the software product will have to communicate with other systems.
	Compliance	The extent to which the software product complies with relevant standards, conventions and regulations.
	Security	The extent to which the software product is able to prevent unauthorized access - intentionally or by accident - to data and software.
	Traceability	The extent to which it can be determined (verified) whether the software product has processed the data correctly.
Usability	Understand ability	The ease with which a user can understand the design, operation and applicability of a software product.
	Learnability	The ease with which a user can understand the design, operation and applicability of a software product.
	Operability	The ease with which the user can get to know the information system.
	Explicitness	The ease with which a user can control an information system and control the resulting results.
	Customisability	The extent to which the product provides clarity in the processing status, such as a progress bar.
	Attractivity	The extent to which the user can customize the system to simplify usage or increase satisfaction.
	Clarity	The degree to which the software product meets latent user requirements, which exceed the actual requirements and wishes.
	Helpfulness	The extent to which the product makes clear what features it offers.
	User-friendliness	The extent to which the product has user instructions to interact with the product.

Table 6-2, Functional quality attributes.

Technical quality attributes

Quality attribute		Description
Technical quality is about the effectiveness of the software product, and the ability to gain insight into the software product and to adjust its operation. The technical quality is important for quickly translating the changing requirements of the business units into software adaptations in the software product.		
Maintainability	Analysability	The ease with which a software product can detect shortcomings or mistakes and the ease with which parts can be modified and analysed.
	Changeability	The ease with which a software product can be modified (to fix errors or to adjust the system to changing circumstances).
	Stability	The extent to which the software product shows unexpected behaviour or errors when changes occur.
	Testability	The ease with which the correct setup and operation of a software product can be established (validated).
	Manageability	The ease with which an owner / manager can ensure that the system is and remains operational (and optimally remains in line with stakeholder expectations).
	Reusability	The extent to which parts of the software product can be used in other information systems.
Portability	Adaptability	The ease with which the software product can be transferred to another hardware / software platform (hardware / software environment) or upgrade to a new version.
	Installability	The ease with which a software product can be installed in the intended environment.
	Conformance	The extent to which the software product adheres to standards or agreements related to portability.
	Replaceability	The ease with which a software product can replace another existing system.

Table 6-3, Technical quality attributes.

IT Infrastructure quality attributes

Quality attribute		Description
The ICT infrastructure quality says something about the availability, capacity and substitutability of the ICT infrastructure.		
Reliability	Maturity	The extent to which the software product is subject to malfunction due to software errors.
	Fault tolerance	The extent to which the software product can maintain a specific performance level in the event of errors in the software or when other systems do not adhere to the interface requirement.
	Recoverability	The ease with which the software product becomes operational again after failure, without (unnoticed) data loss.
	Availability	The extent to which the software product is actually available when the user needs the system.

Quality attribute		Description
	Degradability	The ease with which the system's essential functions can be resumed after a malfunction.

Table 6-4, IT Infrastructure quality attributes.

Service quality attributes

Quality attribute		Description
The operating quality says something about the technically correct operation and efficiency of the software product. Operational quality is important for managing the support of the total ICT infrastructure and delivering high-quality ICT services to the business units.		
Efficiency	Time behaviour	The extent to which the software product needs time to respond to import or to process transactions (and possible high-volume impacts). Examples are response time, transaction speed and speed of batch processing.
	Resource behaviour	The extent to which the software product uses available operational resources (network capacity, disk space, et cetera.).

Table 6-5, Service quality attributes.

6.4 Cloud risk management

In case the quality of a cloud service is not guaranteed, SLA norms will not be met. The extent to which the SLA norms are achieved depends on the extent to which the cloud service provider recognizes and manages the risks. A model that can be used for this purpose is shown in Figure 6-5.

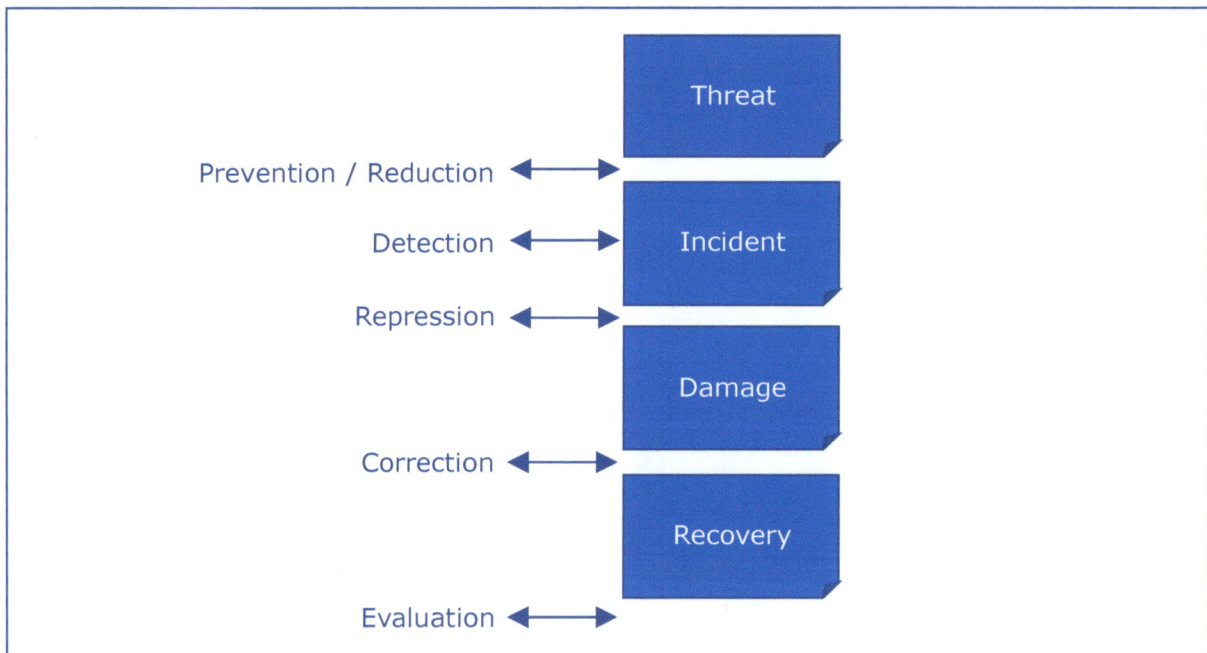

Figure 6-5, Risk management.

As shown in Figure 6-5, the following risk controls are possible.

Prevention / reduction
A threat can be best handled by preventative action or a measure that reduces the consequences. For example, a service threat might be the unavailability of a network connection that is bought as an IaaS service.

A precaution for this unavailability is to buy this IaaS service twice from different cloud service providers. An example of reduction is taking measures to make hacking more difficult. The degree of security determines the extent to which the risk is reduced. Absence of hacking is, however, very difficult or impossible.

Detection
Incidents can be resolved more quickly by detection of disturbance. Thus, there has been no adequate prevention and reduction of the threat did not lead to the prevention of a disturbance. In that case, the best thing to do is to determine the disturbance as early as possible.

Repression
In case there is no adequate detection, an incident will soon be able to cause a lot of damage. In that case, an attempt can be made to limit the damage. This is called repression. An example is to turn off an information system when a virus is detected.

Correction
If repression is not performed or cannot be performed, then it is only possible to repair the damage.

Evaluation
The evaluation serves to determine if the procedures of prevention / reduction, detection, repression and correction need to be adjusted or sharpened.

For the customer, this model can be used by mapping the risks that need to be controlled and determining what types of interventions (measures) can be taken. In addition, the customer must determine which party is deemed to control this risk and to make agreements for it. Otherwise, compliance cannot be determined by means of an audit. Thereafter, a TPA can check whether the cloud service provider actually manages these risks.

The following chapter discusses a standard risk list including the countermeasure(s) that applies to cloud services.

7 Cloud risks

Message:
- Contracts and SLAs are intended to identify and control risks by making the necessary agreements.
- The main classes of risks are successive: contracts (legal aspects), finance, data, functionality, applications and technology.

Reading guideline:
After the introduction (7.1), paragraph 7.2 describes the contractual risks of cloud services. In paragraphs 7.3, 7.4, 7.5, 7.6 and 7.7, the financial, data, functional, application and technical risks are discussed.

7.1 Introduction

D-02

The contracts and SLAs for cloud services are intended to gain control of identified risks. To be able to recognize these risks, a risk analysis must be performed. Some customers cut down this risk analysis due to the lack of knowledge and expertise and fully relate to the cloud services offered by the service provider. However, this is a big pitfall. Because, the customer is always accountable for compliance with legal obligations. In addition, there are always customer specific risks that may not be recognized by the cloud service provider and are therefore not controlled.

The essence of this book on cloud SLAs is therefore about the risks that can be recognized for the various cloud services. These risks can be classified into the following areas of attention:
- R1. contractual risks;
- R2. financial risks;
- R3. data risks;
- R4. functional risks;
- R5. application risks;
- R6. technical risks.

In short, one or more countermeasures are described per risk. A reference is also made to the various check lists for the service management documents which are described in Chapter 13. An overall risk is the reputation damage if the customer of a cloud service cannot correctly and directly account for its own customer, where is what located, how is taken care of et cetera. The transparency that must be achieved with the following measures must also be offered to its own customer if requested.

7.2 Contractual risks

R1.1. The cloud service provider does not allow auditing.
- Request a TPM (SLA 7.7.4).
- Include in the contract an ISAE 3402 audit (SLA 7.7.5).

R1.2 / R1.3 US-EU Safe Harbour does not apply to the SaaS service.
- Include a US-EU Safe Harbour statement in your SaaS (SLA 7.7.6).

R1.4 Cloud service provider can transfer the governance to the customer.
- Explain the governance organization and control explicitly (DAP 5.1).

R1.5 There are international laws and regulations.
- Check the information processing chain (SLA 2.3.2).
- Set requirements for the use of third parties (UC Art 4).
- Requires insight into suppliers (UC Art 4).

R1.6 Legal knowledge is missing.
- Have a lawyer review the contracts periodically (UC Art 20).

R1.7 Distance leads to agreements that are too tight.
- Make agreements on payment termination and signalling instead of stopping (DFA 2.5.2).
- Close monitoring of payments (DFA 2.5.2).

R1.8 Knowledge is insufficient. Include a good Program of Requirements (PoR) and let it review by experts in that field (ESS 1.1).
- Wherever possible, let the cloud service provider audit his services (SLA 7.7.4).
- Involve a cloud service broker.

R1.9 Exit is not possible without tearing up.
- Set an exit strategy (UC Art 16.2).
- Draw up an exit strategy plan (UC Art 16.3).
- Include an escrow clause in the contract (UC Art 16.4).
- Determine the way in which the cloud service provider is unilaterally set aside for bankruptcy and hostile acquisition.
- Prepare for a good insight into the financial health of the cloud service provider.

Exit arrangement standard services
In the event of default services from the cloud service provider, the following exit measurements may be affected:
- Record that customer data must be transferred in the format provided by the customer (UC Art 16.5);
- Record that the cloud service provider destroys data and issues destruction certificate (UC Art 16.6).

Exit arrangement tailor-made services
In case of cloud services provider services, the following exit measurements may be affected:
- record that the cloud service provider documents the service in such a way that it can be taken over by a third party within three months (UC Art 16.7);
- record that the cloud service provider is responsible for ensuring that the service is free of charge if the third party cannot continue the service within the specified three months due to demonstrable defects (UC Art 16.8).

Exit Strategy Steps
The following steps can be taken to achieve a good exit strategy:
- determine the risks of an exit before starting the cloud service provider selection path;
- include a number of mandatory conditions as an option:
  - escrow;
  - data transfer;
  - documentation;
- include some optional conditions as an open question:
  - how is it ensured that after-exit service can be continued by a third party other than data and documentation transfer;
- include conditions in the contract;
- let an annual audit be performed in order to verify that it is possible to exit based on current evidence.

Escrow
Escrow is the safeguarding of critical items that are required for the service of a third party that the customer can claim in the event of a predetermined event occurring. This is useful to apply in case of custom software that is in use by the cloud service provider. This include the following topics: source code, object code, development tools and documentation. The possible consequences of not defining an escrow arrangement in the cloud service contract are:
- additional costs of software and hardware licenses;
- loss of money;
- loss of time;
- customer dissatisfaction;
- breach of contract;
- additional fees for consultant fees, law suits, arbitration fees and lawyers.

The following escrow levels are offered in the market:
- level 1 - inventory & analysis;
- level 2 - compile;
- level 3 - binary comparison;
- level 4 - full usability.

R1.10 Protection of personal data against loss, theft corruption et cetera.
- A cloud service provider must comply with the applicable personal data protection act (SLA 7.7.7).

R1.11 In the cloud, transparency reduces so much that no good risk management is possible.
- The contract must provide transparency. This can be achieved by requiring the right to an audit. This oblige the cloud service provider to use transparent / traceable processing in providing cloud services (SLA 7.7.8).

R1.12 The cloud service provider chain leads to risk of degradation.
- Third party efforts must be communicated to ensure confusion about liability and ownership (gaps or overlaps) (UC Art 4).
- The customer must give permission to allow third parties to operate with the customer's data (UC Art 4). If this permission is not granted by the customer, then the contract may have to be resolved without problems.

7.3 Financial risks

R2.1 The charging strategy is not clear.
- Determine how the cloud service can be settled internally (at the customer) (DFA 2.5.4);
- If possible, agree with the cloud service provider how to charge it internally (DFA 2.5.5).

R2.2 The cloud service appears to be more expensive than the investment costs to do it yourself.
- Determine the scenarios and calculate them in terms of costs, growth et cetera (DFA 2.3.2).
- In any case, take a 3-year calculation period (DFA 2.3.3) at a tender.

R2.3 Total Cost of Ownership (TCO) is not measurable per transaction, user or provided service.
- Determine all direct and indirect costs of cloud services, especially adaptive costs may be higher (DFA 2.3.4).
- Set the cost based on the process, procedure and task demarcation (DFA 2.3.5).
- Require a fully predictable TCO model, so that nowhere hidden costs occur.

R2.4 The costs will increase with the number of users, but do not decrease.
- Explain how the growth and shrinkage of service intake is calculated.

P-05

7.4 Data risks

R3.1 In termination of the contract, loss of data occurs.
- Specify the rights to recover this data (UC Art 16.9)
  - what data?
  - how fast?
  - in what format?

R3.2 The data ownership is not known.
- Data ownership must be claimed and recorded (UC Art 11.2).
- Data usage must be recorded (UC Art 11.3).
- Differentiation can be made in data types such as (UC Art 11.3):
  - business data;
  - metadata;
  - support data.

R3.3 Data may not be located anywhere in the world.
- Contractually disclose the location of the data. Note that having backups in the Netherlands is often an adequate measure (UC 11.5).
- Also include the backup data and monitor data (UC 11.5).

R3.4 Data is not recovered correctly.
- Data recovery requires more than RPO and RTO agreements. Determine in the contract which conditions must be met after a recovery.

R3.5 Responsibility for data quality is not defined (SaaS).
- Set up a list of database tasks and decide who does what e.g.:
  - referential integrity and maintenance business rules (DAP 4.2.2, 4.2.3);
  - correct, full, timely and accurate control data and business data. (DAP 4.2.4);
  - Note: The customer is always accountable for the business data in the cloud.
- Classify the information objects according to CIA and set measures per class (ISS 1.1).

R3.6 Data (transaction) integrity is not guaranteed.
- Request an audit on the solution on aspects such as:
  - Extract Transform Load (ETL) exceptions;
  - Atomicity, Consistency, Isolation, Durability (ACID);
  - error handling;
  - managing dead letter bin (UC R3.9).
- Handle acceptance tests (UC 6.2).
- Agree on repressive measures (ISS 1.1.2).
- Determine a compensation (UC 8.2).

R3.7 No or inadequate exclusivity on various layers.
- Data layer (e.g. shared data) - own database (ISS 1.1.3).

R3.8 Restoring data works differently than expected.
- Perform an audit.
- Agreements of a Disaster Recovery Plan (DRP).
- Agreements about restore testing.
- Execute acceptance tests (DAP 4.2.5, and 4.2.6) / (SLA 3.4.2).

R3.9 It is not known which interfaces there are and how to handle this.
- How does the cloud service provider deal with any interfaces with systems outside its own environment (chains and other forms of integration)? Make agreements on this subject.

7.5 Functional risks

R4.1 Functionality is not properly customizable. Functionality is limited because the SaaS has equal functionality for everyone. There must be space for new service clauses and adjustments to service norms.
- Choose a private cloud or cloud service provider that uses an architecture that allows differentiation per cloud user.
- Determine how customization is charged and what rules are applied in case of custom work.
- Establish an agreement that business rules are customizable / expandable (DAP 4.2.7).

R4.2 The freedom of data processing has been overloaded too much.
- There must be agreements to change volumes (SLA 3.4.3 and DAP4.2.8).
- The ETL errors must be monitored (DAP 4.2.9).
- The manner in which the data is presented must be flexible (online, batch, format, protocol, et cetera. (DAP 4.2.10).
- Business requirements are unique and SaaS solutions are generic. Therefore, the SLA must contain enough space for one-time processing or adjustments and may not be too expensive (SLA 3.4.4 and DAP).
- Data exports must be possible (SLA 3.4.5 and DAP 4.2.12).
- Data streams must be controllable so that incorrect data is rejected (SLA 3.4.6 and DAP 4.2.13).

R4.3 Segregation of duties is not properly regulated.
- The SaaS solution must support task separation to prevent fraud (authorize, control and monitoring) (ESS 1.1.2).
- The SaaS solution must provide a control mechanism to detect fraud (ESS 1.1.3).

R4.4 Cloud supplies jumbles of accounts that are unmanageable.
- Single Sign On (SSO) in the cloud requires specific measures such as a broker service, identity management platforms in the form of a PaaS and federal directory solutions using the content of the on-premise directory structure in the cloud (ESS 1.1.4).

7.6 Application risks

R5.1 No or inadequate exclusivity at application level:
Example: Customer data in a CRM SaaS are directly accessible by other customers of a SaaS service.
- This can be avoided by using an own application runtime of the SaaS (ISS 1.1.5).

R5.2 The recoverability of the application does not meet expectations.
- Application (virtual platform recovery) audit.
- DRP.
- Acceptance test.
- Testing completeness (DAP 4.2.14, 4.2.15, 4.2.16), (UC 6.3).

7.7 Technical risks

R6.1 No or inadequate exclusivity on the network layer (ISS 1.1.7).
Example: Network layer (e.g. Diginotar).
Example: Network is not exclusive.
- Requires its own IP stack, its own IP Local Area Network (LAN) and its own physical network.

R6.2 The recoverability of technology cannot be trusted (SLA 6.2, DAP4.2.17):
Example: Network layer (recovery settings).
- Require an audit.
- Require a DRP.
- Require a PEN test.

R6.3 The risk of hacking is greater in a cloud (ISS 1.1.8).
Other customers make it interesting to hack the provider, causing low risk profile customers suddenly get more risk of being hacked.
- Use a private cloud.

R6.4 Through the virtualization in a PaaS, a customer can shut down himself without having access to PaaS services.
- For the risk of firewall blocking, backdoor capability may be required as a countermeasure (ISS 1.1.9).
- For the risk of no longer being visible to physical objects, the use of local support may be required (DAP 4.2.18).

R6.5 The environment is not properly monitored, resulting in consequential damage to the customer.
- In case the monitoring is less transparent and there is no right of inspection, the countermeasure is to require inspection rights in case of hacking or disturbance (DAP 5.4.2).
- Monitoring of access computer centre, application, data and data mutation must be due (DAP 5.4.3).

R6.6 Cloud solutions use generic solutions that do not cover your own risks.
- Auditing, e.g., Payment Card Industry (PCI) Data Security Standard (DSS) must ensure risks (SLA 7.7.9);

- In case of a risk that the security of the platform is not water tight, a PEN test must be required (DAP 4.2.19);
- In case of a restriction of supported operating systems, which means that applications cannot be hosted, a representative acceptance test must be performed (ISS 1.10).

R6.7 The virtualization of cloud solutions is so complex that no-one knows what the effects on the physical level are. This applies to SaaS, PaaS and IaaS combinations. This also applies to the use of subnets, which makes it difficult to determine what is virtual and what is not virtual.

R6.8 The infrastructure underlying the SaaS solution is not to be trusted.
Examples are:
- Limitation of traffic in protocols (ESS 1.1.5).
  - Perform an acceptance test that tests the required protocols.
- Scalability bandwidth (ESS 1.1.6).
  - Perform a load test and test if the network is scalable.
- Too much traffic through the network (ESS 1.1.7).
  - Analyse the bandwidth from the customer to the cloud service provider to prevent bottlenecks.
  - Perform a load test that minimizes the expected load test.
- QoS is not adjustable or not flexible (ESS 1.1.8, DAP 4.2.1).
  - Perform a test to test different QoS service levels.
- Logical network is not secure (ESS 1.1.9, ISS 1.1.11).
  - Perform a PEN test.

R6.9 Internet security possibilities are limited. Everything is connected to the Internet and therefore always hackable.
- Check the SLA for a correct CIA rating (SLA 3.4.9, ISS1.1.10).

R6.10 Customer and cloud service provider's identity management solution does not connect well.
- Consider a directory federation service for authentication (E1.1.11).
- Analyse the identity management strategy (authentication and authorization) for possible failures and connection problems.

R6.11 A PaaS based on a third-party IaaS provides additional security risks to the customer (ESS 1.1.12, DAP 4.2.22).
- Requires insight into subcontractors.

8 Cloud SLA's

Message:
- A cloud SLA contains many aspects of a regular SLA. Important aspects are the countermeasures of risks that the customer wants to cover.
- Each cloud pattern has its own pallet of risks. It is important to keep this in mind when composing a SLA.

Reading guideline:
In section 8.1, the subjects are nominated that should be included in a cloud SLA. Section 8.2 contains a SLA template incorporating the SLA topics. Topics that require specific attention are red-coloured. In addition, an explanation is given per subject in section 8.3. In section 8.4, the subjects of an Under-Pinning Contract (UC) are formulated and the UC template and UC notes are defined, respectively in paragraphs 8.5 and 8.6, respectively.

8.1 SLA subjects

The following topics are usually included in a SLA:
- Document management
- Definitions
- Goal
- Subject of the agreement
- Parties, declaration and signature
- Start and maturity
- Service description
- Performance agreements
- Performance indicators and performance norms
- Reporting, meeting and tuning
- Accountability and control

8.2 SLA template

Below is a chapter layout of a SLA.

1. General
    1.1 Subject of the agreement
    1.2 Parties, declaration and signature
    1.3 Purpose of the SLA
    1.4 Commencement and maturity
    1.5 Concepts
    1.6 Related documents
    1.7 Service description
    1.8 Performance obligation
    1.9 Control and governance
    1.10 Service opening hours and service maintenance times
    1.11 Work agreements and procedures
    1.12 Document management

2 Description of service
    2.1 Introduction
    2.2 General description of the service
    2.3 Service description
    2.4 Environments

3 Performance Agreements
    3.1 Introduction
    3.2 Product performance indicators
    3.3 Process performance indicators

8.3 SLA template explanation

1 General

This chapter discusses a number of topics related to the cloud service and the agreement.

This chapter should clarify the purpose, context and content of the cloud service. By naming the parties and the manner of cooperation, an impression is also given how the way in which this document is positioned.

1.1 Subject agreement

The subject of the agreement must be clearly appointed and the used terms must be clearly and unambiguously defined in the SLA.

1.2 Parties, statement and signature

This topic is usually included in the SLA and refers to the entire SLA.

It is possible to link to this agreement a number of points that are of importance. These are then taken under the heading "Consider that:". It is recommended not to include a whole list of items that are separate subjects such as SLA's duration and maintenance. This makes the SLA concise but not clear because the subjects don´t appear properly in the bullets.

1.3 Purpose van de SLA

T-07

The purpose of a SLA is one of the subjects that is well-known in small SLAs. In many SLAs, in general the purpose of a SLA is generally included, such as "The purpose of this document is to capture service agreements in measurable performance agreements so that accountability can be taken."

This purpose adds little value because it is the generic goal that already involves the management of a SLA. The intention is to establish a purpose that is the reason why it was chosen to handle the SLA. The purpose must therefore indicate the SLA business case. In other words, what's wrong if we do not use a SLA for this intended service.

Thus, there are several purposes for a SLA. Over time, the purpose can also change. If time comes to cut back, it may be that the purpose becomes to be more efficient. The content of the SLA will therefore be more focused on reducing the required service management effort.

P-06

The purpose of the SLA has to have an impact on the content of the SLA in order to realize the business case. Examples are:
- The purpose of this SLA is to permanently adjust the service to the changing needs of the business;
- The purpose of this SLA is to make agreements about service provisioning to give the customer a steering wheel to better tune the service to the needs of the business;
- The purpose of this SLA is to make the ICT department more customer oriented in thinking and acting;
- The purpose of this SLA is to provide administrative information provisioning so that management can better control the ICT department;
- The purpose of this SLA is to improve the competitiveness of the customer organization;
- The purpose of this SLA is to improve the effectiveness and / or efficiency of business processes.

For a SLA that concerns a public SaaS solution, this section will not add or hardly add value because it will be the same for all customers. The purpose is then to clarify the customer for which he has chosen.

1.4 Start and duration

The duration of a SLA is usually one year. The start of the SLA is usually equal to the start of a budget period. This is usually the same as the calendar year. The advantage of this is that the budget of services can be taken evenly into the annual budget round. In case a SLA is linked to a contract, the start and duration term of the SLA is usually related to that of the contract.

1.5 Terminology

T-08

This section defines all specific definitions. Often reference is made to a central document containing the definitions or to another document such as the service catalogue.

1.6 Related documents

It is important to indicate which documents are related to the SLA. In any case, there is often a service catalogue or a DAP. If the SLA is related to a contract, it is important to include the rank order arrangement. This arrangement applies if there is contradiction between documents. The rank order arrangement determines which documents are leading. For example, the following rank order arrangement often occurs:
- terms and conditions;
- contract;
- SLA;
- DAP.

If something is agreed in the SLA that contradicts the terms and conditions, then the terms and conditions will apply unless the contradiction is explicitly approved.

1.7 Service description

The services are described in the service catalogue.

It is not the intended that these be reformulated in the SLA. However, specific items per service can be defined in the SLA.

1.8 Result obligation

There are two possibilities to make agreements about the service, namely a performance obligation and a commitment obligation. In case of a commitment, the cloud service provider must deliver to the customer what has been agreed. In the Netherlands, a best effort is a soft ground agreement, with SLA norms being valid as a guideline, but not being complied with. The deviations from the SLA norms are often not culpable. Outside of the Netherlands however, the best effort clause is interpreted differently and is almost equivalent to a result obligation. In case of dispute, the cloud service provider must provide proof of actual effort. But also with a result obligation, we must look carefully at the wording. This can be specified so strictly that it is hardly possible to speak of a result obligation. This includes any disclaimers, boundary conditions or requirements imposed on the customer by the cloud service provider.

1.9 Monitoring and control

There are essentially three approaches to monitoring the service norms, namely reactive, proactive and predictive. The reactive monitoring means that the incident management process investigates the deviations of SLA norms. However, by providing a good monitoring facility, it is possible to see an incident in advance. This form of SLA monitoring is called proactive. An even further form of SLA monitoring can be achieved by simulating future-expected workload. This can, for example, be translated into the services based on a forecasted increase in business activities of the business processes. This form of SLA monitoring is called predictive.

1.10 Service opening time and service maintenance time

It is common for all services to agree on the support time, technical opening hours, maintenance time. The support time is the time the customer can use the service and get support when using the service. This includes a service desk and / or a standby service, so that questions are answered and incidents are solved. This is in contrast to the technical opening time at which the customer can reduce service but no support is possible. The maintenance time is the time when the services are not available to the customer because maintenance work must be performed on the infrastructure or application(s).

Finally, the batch processing needs to be considered. If the on-line users cannot work during batch processing, batch processing should also take place during maintenance.

1.11 Work agreements and procedures

In order to realize the service norms, various agreements are required. These agreements are often included in a separate document, namely the DAP. The reason for breaking these agreements from the norms is to ensure that the signed SLA remains unchanged if the DAP agreements are to be modified. The approval and signing of a DAP is in practice much quicker to handle because it only concerns the process and not the service norms. Of course, the DAP adjustment may affect the cost of service (DFA), performance agreements (SLA) and possibly contractual agreements (UC).

1.12 Document management

Document management includes various aspects that need to be addressed, namely:
- modification and termination of the SLA and the consequences for related documents;
- with whom changes need to be notified;
- who makes changes;
- who should approve changes;
- digital version.

2. Description of service

The services are described in detail in the service catalogue. This chapter in the SLA is only intended to outline the service.

2.1 Introduction

Brief explanation of this chapter in the SLA.

2.2 General description of the service

In particular, the consistency of decreased services and deviations from the standard service grant are described in this section. This chapter of the SLA has not yet entered into substantive agreements.

2.3 The service description

Often, emphasis is placed in the SLA on service levels and performance indicators without properly defining the services and relevant management domains to which the SLA relates. In a SLA, they should be defined as clear as possible.

Describing the service based on the management domains concerned gives a clear definition of the SLA. This can be achieved by defining the domains of the parties involved, such as those of the cloud service broker, the cloud service provider, the suppliers and the customer.
If the cloud service provider delivers a SaaS solution, the subcontractors can be a PaaS and IaaS cloud service provider.

2.4 The environments

The various environments that are being offered should be defined like the production environment, acceptance environment, test environment, development environment, experimental environment, continuity environment, shadow environment, training environment et cetera. All the more because the service norms are often different for each environment.

P-08

3. Performance agreements

The agreements in the SLA depend on the cloud pattern. An IaaS, PaaS and SaaS have different performance agreements.

3.1 Introduction

An IaaS, PaaS and SaaS SLA will generally only be based on a product view or service view. Each view leads to another set of performance agreements in the form of performance indicators. The process view and governance view are not applicable. This because the cloud service provider's processes are not visible to the customer. The governance view is only relevant to the cloud service provider for the management of its services.

3.2 Product performance indicators

The products are described in the product catalogue, often as part of the service catalogue. The SLA only nominates the performance that will be delivered around the product. Especially the IaaS services are product oriented. SaaS services are mainly service-oriented.

3.3 Process performance indicators

The agreements about the service management processes are often recorded in the form of a service, such as the service desk opening hours or the handling of a call. These services around the service management processes are usually included in the service catalogue. The SLA contains only the agreements in this regard.

3.4 Service performance indicators

Of course, service agreements are also included in the service catalogue and only the norms are agreed here. Examples are the availability and performance norms of a SaaS service.

4. Service report

This chapter describes the agreements on the reports.

4.1 Introduction

Briefly, this section explains the different types of reports. In addition, two types of distinctions are known as lead reports and lag reports. Lead reports provide direct control of service such as lead time per incident or change. The lag reports provide a retrospective control based on aggregated data.

4.2 Lead report

These reports are usually offered online so that timeliness is as high as possible.

Service portals include insight into the status of activities such as incidents and changes.

4.3 lag report
The lag reporting is usually a monthly report that is used in the operational service meeting. In doing so, it is checked whether certain SLA norms have not been met and what has been done or done.

5. Communication
This chapter describes the communication lines (communication matrix), escalation and meeting structures that are necessary for the service level management process to run well.

5.1 Introduction
Brief introduction to this chapter.

5.2 Operational meeting
The purpose of the operational meeting is to evaluate the service norms (usually per month) with the customer which service norms have not been met and which ones not. Topics are incidents, problems and changes. During the operational meeting, the cloud service provider, a representative of the user organization and the client are in any event involved. In case of a public SaaS service, the operational service meeting usually does not take place.

5.3 Escalation meeting
In case of escalation due to serious disturbances in the contracted service, the cloud service provider initiates an escalation meeting. If requested, a meeting is initiated at the customer's request. Here too, the relevant agreements are as described in the DAP.

5.4 Evaluation new SLA
Usually after three months after the start of the agreement, the cloud service provider and the customer evaluate the SLA agreements based on the findings from the service meeting in order to adjust them if necessary.

5.5 Tactical meeting
The tactical meeting is intended to evaluate the agreed service norms with the customer. The monthly reports serve as input for these meetings. It discusses which deviations have been observed and which actions are deactivated to prevent repetition. New developments in both demand and supply are also being looked into. This is a meeting of usually once a quarter. There are no major adjustments of the SLA expected on a quarterly basis. Once a year, the SLA is re-evaluated and modified and renewed if desired. In this meeting, at least the service level manager and the client are present.

5.6 Strategic meeting
The strategic meeting is intended to evaluate the portfolio of services and products. Important participants are the client, the relevant architects, the ICT manager and the service level manager.

5.7 Participants in the service meeting
An overview of participants in the service meeting should be defined in the DAP. The location of the meeting must also be determined, as well as who makes out the minutes of this meeting.

5.8 Contact persons, Responsible persons and addresses
The DAP requires an overview of:
- contacts and responsible for the mutual relationship;
- contacts and responsible persons in escalation and / or accidents;
- overview of visit and postal addresses of affected organizations and locations.

6 Mutual obligations
For cloud SLAs, it is important to look at the mutual obligations. Reference can be made to the general terms and conditions and contractual obligations.

In addition, this chapter often also includes business as the performance of the work and the provision of information about the provided services aspects.

6.1 Introduction
Brief introduction to this chapter.

6.2 Operation
It is important to include the general obligation in the SLA next to a very detailed description. An example of this is the agreement of the cloud service provider's responsibility for operational management for the environments offered. The agreement of the responsibility of conducting reviews, audits and participation in meeting also includes.

6.3 Information
The customer should be provided timely with information about the service. For example, scheduled maintenance should be communicated in a timely manner. Also, information on procedural and organizational changes is also included.

6.4 Occupation staff
An important factor in meeting the SLA norms is in the occupation of the staff. In case of external service, agreements can be made regarding the number of employees, the level of education and the relevant certifications.

6.5 Good home paternity
A cloud service provider will generally not make agreements regarding good home paternity because a remote service is provided. However, agreements can be made about things like dealing with information and passwords.

6.6 Legal frameworks
It is important to indicate which legal frameworks apply to the service provisioning.

7 Terms and Conditions
This chapter describes the terms and conditions under which the services are provided. This chapter also describes how to deal with disputes, standards and rules, copyright, software licenses and secrecy.

7.1 Limitations, Dependencies and Force Majeure
SLA norms can only be realized in reasonableness and fairness. This means that there are justified reasons why the SLA is not being met. This applies both to a SLA with a commitment and result obligation. The categories of these reasons are limitations, dependencies and force majeure. For example, a restriction may be that a particular category of products is not supported. For example, dependence on a subcontractor of the customer with whom no contract has been concluded and the customer does not want to change. Force majeure is located in external sources that cannot be tackled such as hurricanes, earthquakes and other uncontrollable external causes that adversely affect service.

7.2 Disputes
In contracts, the concept of dispute is a legal charge. However, in a SLA, the dispute is limited to a difference of opinion between the customer and the cloud service provider on operational matters. The SLA must describe how the discussion about this disagreement can be scanned.

7.3 Norms and standards
If the SLA has to provide an externally defined standard framework such as NEN 7510, it is important to indicate this in the SLA. The SLA and related documents must explicitly state in this regard.

7.4 Copyright
In SLAs that belong to contracts, agreements are made about the copyright. The copyright relates mainly to the software products and the accompanying documentation that the customer may use.

7.5 Software licences
In SLAs that are contractually bound, clear agreements must be made about who is responsible for granting software licenses. In that case, a report must also be provided stating that these licenses have been paid. This is important to prevent negative publications about illegal software. Additionally, non-payment of software licenses may result in unavailability of the service.

7.6 Confidentiality
Agreements on confidentiality are made in SLAs that are contractual. The confidentiality concerns agreements on information (organization, operation, files), publication (agreement), legislation (personal data protection act) and staff (compliancy).

7.7 Accountability
There should be agreements about the frequency of accountability and the control thereof. For example, the legislature proposes personal registration and financial reporting to organizations. The compliance with this legal obligation by the customer does not end when a service is bought from an internal or external provider. Therefore, a provider must be accountable to the customer showing that he has adhered to the frameworks as stipulated by law.

In addition, the customer can provide additional requirements to the cloud service provider to ensure that business critical risks such as continuity, availability and reputation are governed. To this end, agreements must be made regarding both the frequency of accountability and the verification of the accuracy of such accountability.

Appendix 1: Change register
This appendix contains the changes made during the term of the SLA. This makes it possible to understand what the adjustments have been. As a result, the document does not have to be completely redesigned and signed of at a minor change.

Appendix 2: Under-pinning contracts
This appendix describes the Under-pinning Contracts (UC) of this SLA.

8.4 UC subjects
The following topics are usually included in a UC:
- Liability
- Terms and Conditions
- Payments
- Prices, bonus / malus
- Non-competition clause
- Billing information, payment period, VAT
- Warranty
- Confidentiality
- Intellectual (ownership) rights / adjustments
- Legal acceptance procedure
- Transfer
- Force majeure, dissolution, disputes committee
- Ranking order arrangement
- Insurance
- Merger clause

8.5 UC template
Below is a chapter layout of a UC. The paragraphs that require specific attention are red-coloured.

1 General
  1.1 Objective
  1.2 Related documents

2 Structure of the contract
  2.1 Date of commencement of contract

2.2 Maintenance of the contract
Article 1. Glossary
Article 2. Object of agreement
Article 3. Duration of the agreement
Article 4. Cooperation by the parties
Article 5. Delivery
Article 6. Acceptance
Article 7. Warranty
Article 8. Liability
Article 9. Prices, bonus / malus
Article 10. Payments
Article 11. Intellectual (proprietary) rights
Article 12. Confidentiality and Security
Article 13. Insurance
Article 14. Transfer of rights and obligations
Article 15. Force majeure
Article 16. Dissolution
Article 17. Disputes, applicable law and forum choice
Article 18. The provision of services
Article 19. General
Article 20. Other

8.6 UC template explanation

1 General

1.1 goal
Goal of the contract

1.2 Related documents

T-09

A contract often relates to various documents, such as the terms and conditions, the SLA and so on. It is important to name them all. In addition, the rank order must be determined. It has to be determined which document goes beyond the other in case of contradictions. Usually, the terms are of a higher order than the SLA.

2 Structure of the contract
The contract consists mainly of articles. In order to get these articles legally "watertight", a conceptual framework is indispensable. This chapter defines these terms, supplemented with other contract-related information.

2.1 Date of entry contract
The date of entry and term of the contract must be defined. This is usually one year with a tacit renewal and notice period.

2.2 Maintenance of the contract
Contract management must be familiar with how changes can be made, who processes them in the document and how they are declared valid.

Article 1. Glossary
The glossary of a contract is usually much more extensive and more legally worded than that of a SLA. Often terms are closely related to each other, so that whole chains of references arise. In addition, the conceptual framework contains additional legal terms such as: liability, payment term, warranty, notice of default, dissolution and so on.

Article 2. Object of agreement
This article describes the services to which the contract relates. Reference can be made to the SLA or the service catalogue.

Article 3. Duration of the agreement

The term of the contract is defined or related to a higher document such as a mantle contract. A mantle contract is applied if a cloud service provider has accommodated all general provisions in one central contract.

Article 4. Cooperation by the parties

Aspects identified in this Article are the mutual obligations regarding notification, support, third party engagement, contact points and information disclosure. Especially with a SaaS solution, it is important to look closely at the use of a PaaS and IaaS cloud service provider. This is especially true in relationship to the security such as access to data.

Article 5. Delivery

Delivery concerns the delivery date, compatibility, manageability, license fees, escrow arrangement, and hardware adjustments. For licensing rights, it is important to note that the cloud service provider is responsible for deciding which licensing rights are linked to the delivery, or to exclude them. The escrow arrangement states that the cloud service provider secures the source code and object code to a third party. The customer is entitled to this software in case the cloud service provider fails or is declared bankrupt. In case of a cloud service, a third party can also be chosen to ensure that the service is delivered after disconnection by the cloud service provider.

Article 6. Acceptance

The acceptance includes agreements on the initial first acceptance, acceptance process, acceptance test, acceptance report, handling of small defects, recovery of defects, second acceptance, contract termination, acceptance date, defects to be remedied, lost software, quality control, demonstration and exclusion of recovery. Especially with a SaaS solution, the question is to what extent there is an acceptance. Is there for example an acceptance environment?

Article 7. Warranty

This article contains the terms of the warranty period, the determination of functionality and quality, recovery of defects, registration procedure, response time, diagnosis & repair time, program denominations, access, right of recovery, compatibility, portability, exclusion old versions, exclusion data loss, exclusion unauthorized changes, exclusions specification changes and exclusion external cause. Important for cloud services is to make agreements regarding data quality guarantee and recovery in case of data loss or mutilation.

Article 8. Liability

The liability includes the terms of notice, liability statement, damages, consequential loss, damage to delivery, exclusions, professional errors and maximum liability. Important aspects of a cloud service are the agreements on compensation and liability for licenses.

Article 9. Prizes, bonus / malus

This article describes the applicable VAT, the price guarantee and the price of the service and / or products to be delivered. Additionally, a bonus / malus arrangement may be included in this article. In view of the confidentiality of the financial agreements and the ease of maintenance, these topics can be split into a DFA. With the cloud services, it is important to pay attention to the prices. The price is often calculated on the basis of a decrease. This may over time be higher than the alternatives to the SaaS solution.

Article 10. Payments

Agreements for the payments are made on billing, billing information, payment terms, settlement, overdue payment periods and the exclusion of incorrect invoices. These aspects can also be included in a DFA.

Article 11. Intellectual (property) rights

This article describes the exclusions of the right to customer customization, the preservation of property rights, the exclusions of intellectual property rights and the safeguarding of claims.

Cloud solutions need to be made especially on the dates and format in which the data is delivered in case of a contract termination. This applies not only to the transactional data but also to the master data, metadata, control parameters and service management data. Master data concerns data such as customer data. Metadata is the definition of data and integrity rules. Control parameters are the norms that are assigned to business rules such as VAT rates. Service management data is information such as incidents, problems, and changes that are recorded in the cloud service provider's service management systems. Also, aspects, such as the location of the data are important. Other aspects concern the agreements about exclusivity and destruction of the hardware.

Article 12. Confidentiality and Security
Both parties make agreements on the confidentiality and security of information, the publication thereof, compliance with legislation, compliancy with security procedures and security agreements.

Article 13. Insurance
Agreements are made regarding the liability.

Article 14. Transfer of rights and obligations
The transfer of rights and obligations determines to what extent the customer has the right to offer or license the services provided to third parties.

Article 15. Force majeure
This article sets the deadline for the customer to dissolve the contract as a result of non-delivery by the cloud service provider due to force majeure. In addition, this article appoints the disturbances of the service that in any event do not lead to force majeure such as: lack of staff, strikes, staff illness, abandonment or malfunction of materials or software, malfunction of third party enabled third party service providers and / or liquidity or solvency problems on the part of supplier.

Article 16. Dissolution
Both parties agree on the terms under which the contract can be terminated. In addition, it identifies which mutual obligations continue to exist, such as indemnity for violation of intellectual property rights, secrecy, insurance coverage cession, dispute resolution, applicable law, domicile choice and liability matters. Important aspects include the exit strategy and escrow arrangement.

Article 17. Disputes, applicable law and forum choice
This article describes the application of a particular arbitration, the determination of the non-binding advice, the definition of dispute, the analysis, the solution, the advice of the committee, the escalation, the costs and the determination of Dutch law.

Article 18. The provision of services
The description of the service. Possibly, this content may be split into a SLA that is binding on the contract.

Article 19. General
Finally, the contract includes an article containing general articles on the scope, compliance, staff (non-competition clause), fine, merger clause and terms of the cloud service provider. The scope concerns the determination that what has been agreed and formulated in this document. This provision is in line with the merger clause that excludes claims made on prior agreements and that only the contract is binding. The determination of the staff concerns the exclusion of the acquisition of each other's staff for a certain period of time. The determination of compliance relates inter alia to the way in which oral notices, commitments or agreements are not legally declared valid.

9 Cloud governance

Message:
- Cloud governance is an essential aspect of cloud services. On the one hand, the concept of cloud services eliminates the customer through risks by effectively controlling and managing an external party. On the other hand, governance significantly limits the customer's capabilities.
- In advance, the customer needs to consider very well what degree of governance is desired. Once the cloud service provider is chosen, the service is usually poured into concrete.

Reading guideline:
In paragraph 9.1, the principles of governance are briefly described. Section 9.2 describes the possibilities of governance with a cloud service provider.

9.1 What is governance?

Cloud governance includes the control model that makes it possible to get hold of the services provided by cloud service providers. To this end, the concept of service should first be described. ITIL 2011 describes a service based on the service assets as shown in Figure 9-1.

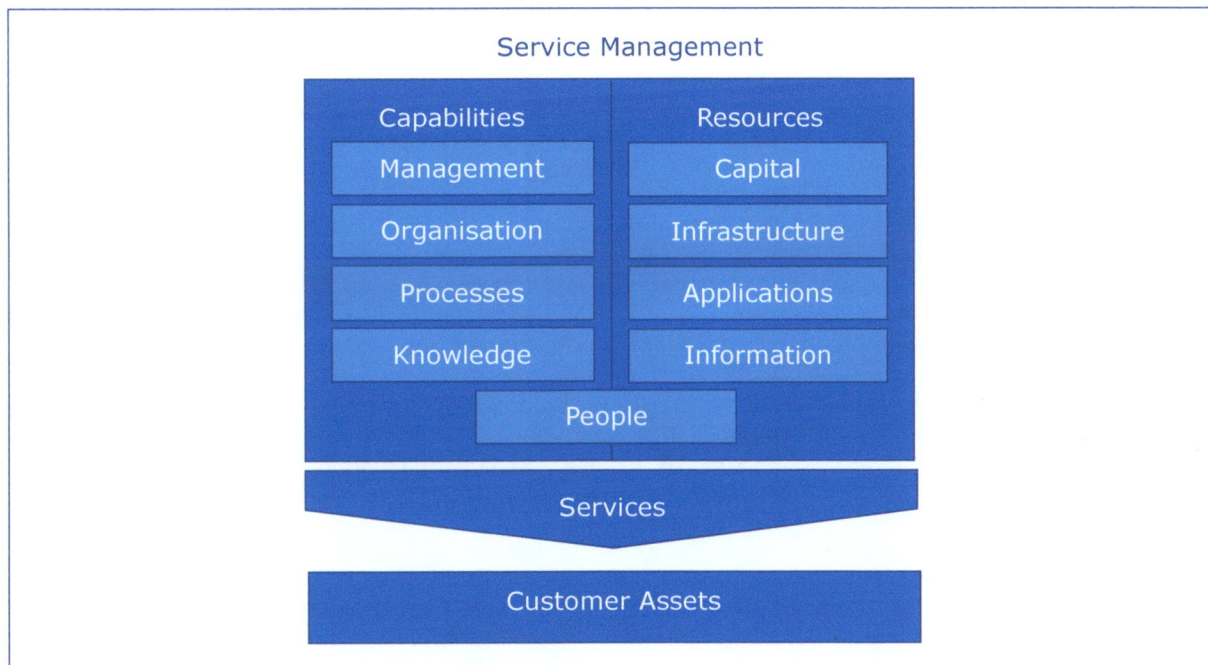

Figure 9-1, Service assets conform ITIL 2011.

A service consists of capabilities and resources. These are defined as follows.

Capability:
Capability is the ability of an organization, person, process, application, Configuration Item (CI) or ICT service to perform an activity. It's an organization's intangible assets.

Resources:
Resource is a common term for resources, including ICT infrastructure, people, capital or other things that help to provide the ICT service. Resources are considered as (tangible) assets of an organization.

The capabilities and resources are the service assets of an ICT service that adds value to the customer.

> **Service assets:**
> A service asset is any resource or capability of a service provider. The service assets include everything that can contribute to providing a customer service by the cloud service provider. Within ITIL 2011, the following classes of service assets are recognized: management, organization, processes, knowledge, capital, infrastructure, applications, information and people.

The governance on a service involves steering the cloud service provider in order to support business processes (horizontal business alignment) and, on the other, to realize the line organization goals (vertical business alignment). The horizontal alignment is expressed in closing a SLA. In this, the business provides services with which performance norms should be provided to support business processes in order to realize the goals of business processes. This can, for example, be guaranteed by processing a certain amount of transactions in a certain amount of time. The vertical business alignment involves supporting the SLA from achieving business goals that are determined by the line organization in, for example, a balanced scorecard.

9.2 What is cloud governance?

The cloud service provided by the cloud service provider provides a (partial) completion of the service assets that are normally filled in by the customer. For example, an IaaS ensures that the customer does not have to worry about the infrastructure. This is delivered in the form of a service. The PaaS service further implements the infrastructure service such as providing an authorization and authentication service. The SaaS solution also replaces the application service assets at the customer, together with the infrastructure assets.

In addition to resource assets such as infrastructure and application assets, the cloud service provider also performs the capabilities needed to deploy resource assets in accordance with the established SLA norms. At a SaaS, the cloud service provider provides a full completion of all assets and provides the service based on a black box management.

The latter is now exactly the limiting factor of a cloud service solution. The customer has no influence on the capabilities and resources that are being used for the company's own business processes. With a public SaaS solution, only interfacing controls can be limited to the generic agreements that the cloud service provider delivers by default and any specific agreements as far as the public service permits.

Controlling a SaaS service is therefore limited. This also limits the flexibility of business processes. It is therefore important to think carefully about it, to take measures and to make agreements with the service provider. This makes the risks identified in Chapter 13 all the more important.

9.3 Fulfilment of governance?

When choosing a cloud solution, it is important to gain an understanding of the service management processes. Any link between customer and service provider is indeed a possible point of regulation on which agreements should be made.

Figure 9-2 shows three columns. The first column is the user organization that can execute certain tasks of functional management such as that of a super user for the user support process. The second column is the service management organization that purchases service such as a SaaS, PaaS or IaaS. And the third column is the cloud service provider that provides the relevant service.

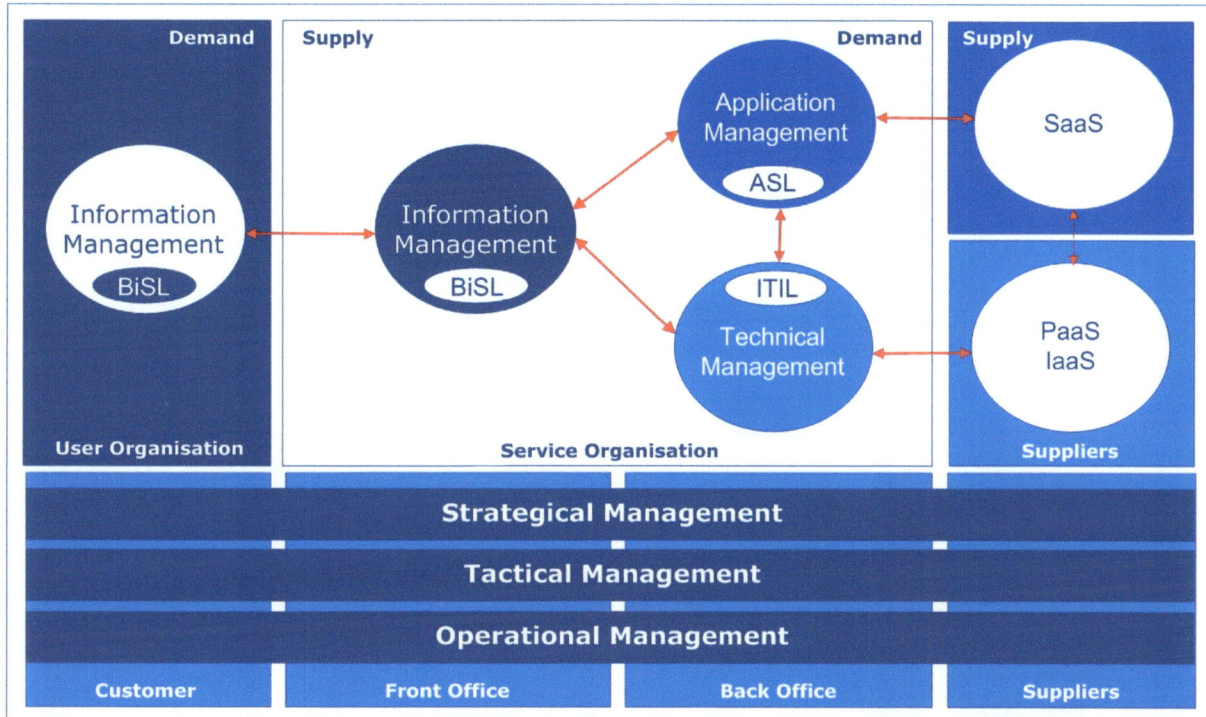

Figure 9-2, Service management domains.

In this respect, it is important to identify the level of service management processes in the form of a blueprint, as depicted in Figure 9-3, by level (strategy, tactics and operational). This figure is just an example of organizing processes. Each organization may choose its own layout.

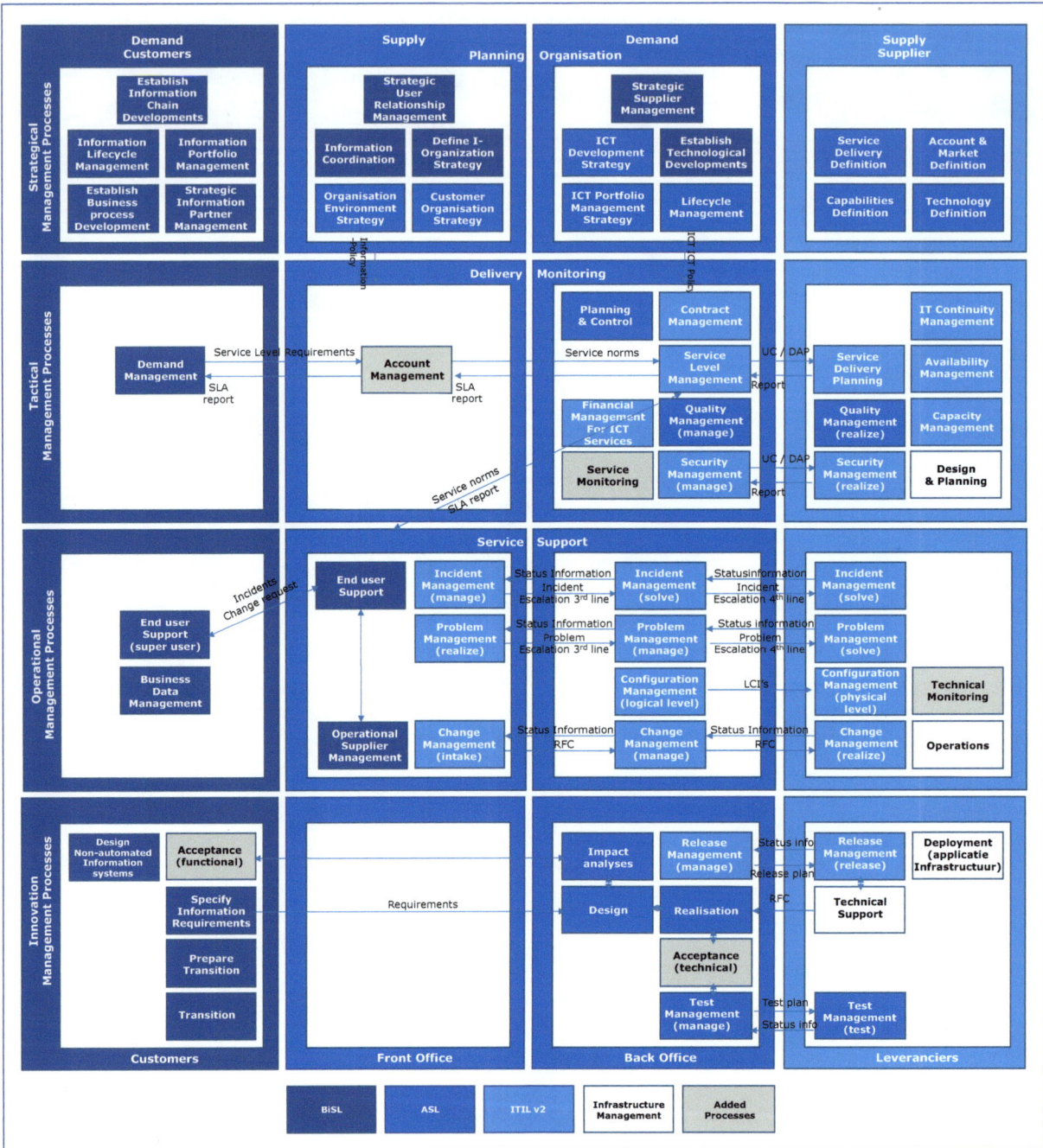

Figure 9-3, Processes per service management domain.

Of importance to the cloud SLA is that each service management process selects which domain it will be and whether there is an interface with a cloud service provider. This is also called the process demarcation. For each process, partly completed by the customer's organization and by the cloud service provider, a procedure demarcation must be established as shown in Figure 9-4 for the incident management process.

If the cloud service provider already has a standard cloud SLA and DAP, it is important to analyse what impact this has on its own service management processes. For example, the cloud service provider does not mention tactical processes such as information security management, capacity management and availability management.

The question is then whether the cloud service provider can handle the volume of transactions during peak moments and whether the data security is guaranteed. The cloud service provider does not obviously disagree with this quality with the customer. More information about the format of processes per management domain is described in "SLA best practices" [BEST 2013].

The process and procedure demarcation is very difficult with public SaaS services. The cloud service provider offers a public service that is similar for all customers. In this case, the demarcation is more a risk analysis tool than a reconciliation of SLA agreements.

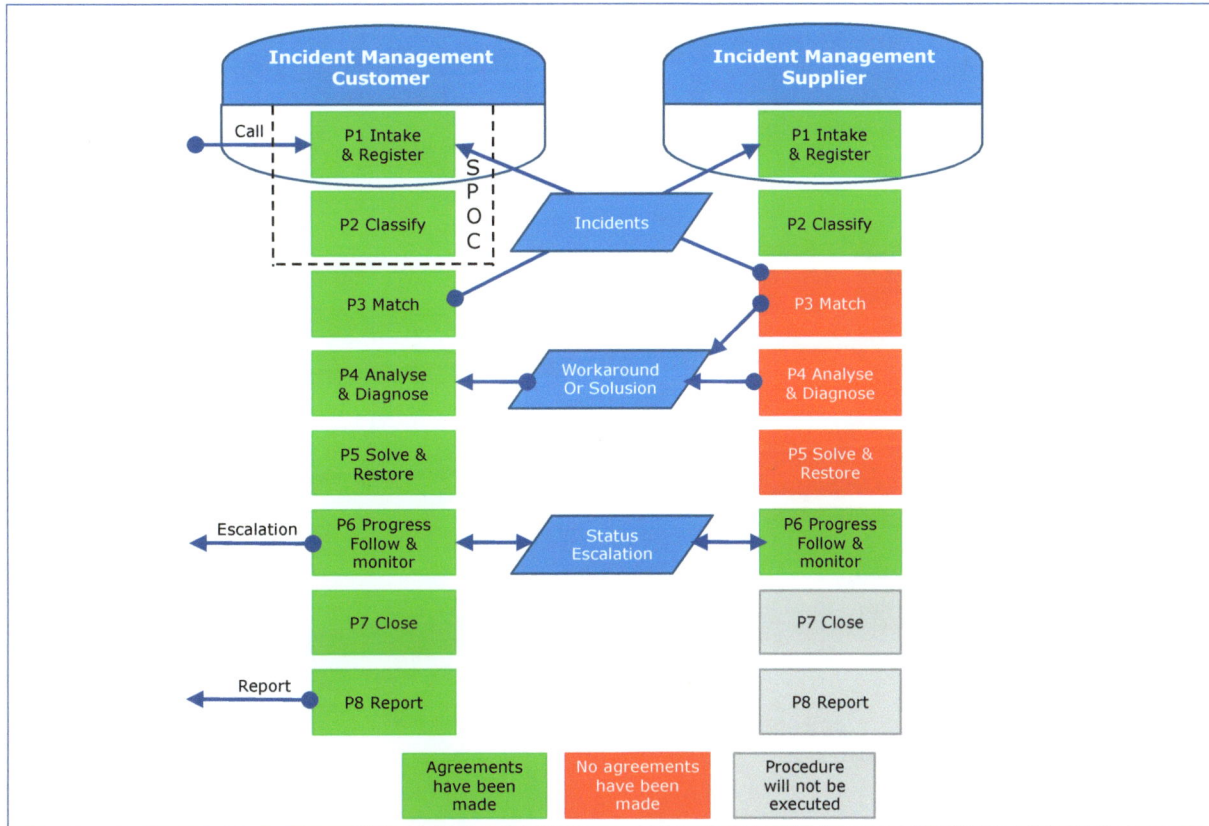

Figure 9-4, Procedure demarcation.

10 Cloud SLA-measurements

Message:
- There are various possibilities to make the SLA norms measurable. Any kind of monitoring has its pros and cons.
- The service level manager must be familiar with the monitor architectures and, per monitor architecture, know which aspects are not measured. These are the potential aspects of unreliable SLA reports.

Reading guideline:
The introduction (10.1) describes the various monitor architectures. Sections 10.2 to 10.6 describe the service desk, built-in, component-based, End User eXperience (EUX) and Real User Monitoring (RUM) monitor architectures. Subsequently, paragraph 10.7 describes the do's and don'ts, followed by a conclusion (10.8) and summary (10.9).

10.1 Introduction

Making service agreements on an ICT service requires that the stated service norms be monitored. Over time, various methods and techniques have been developed for this purpose. Each solution has specific advantages and disadvantages. This chapter provides an overview of commonly used solutions for monitoring ICT services.

In Figure 10-1, the monitor layer model is recorded. This model is based on the monitor model as published in "Beheren onder Architectuur" [Best 2017]. This model shows that measuring instruments can be monitored at various levels to monitor SLAs. This section briefly describes the monitor functions in Figure 10-1. A more detailed description of these functions can be found in the book "Ketenbeheer in de Praktijk" [Best 2015b].

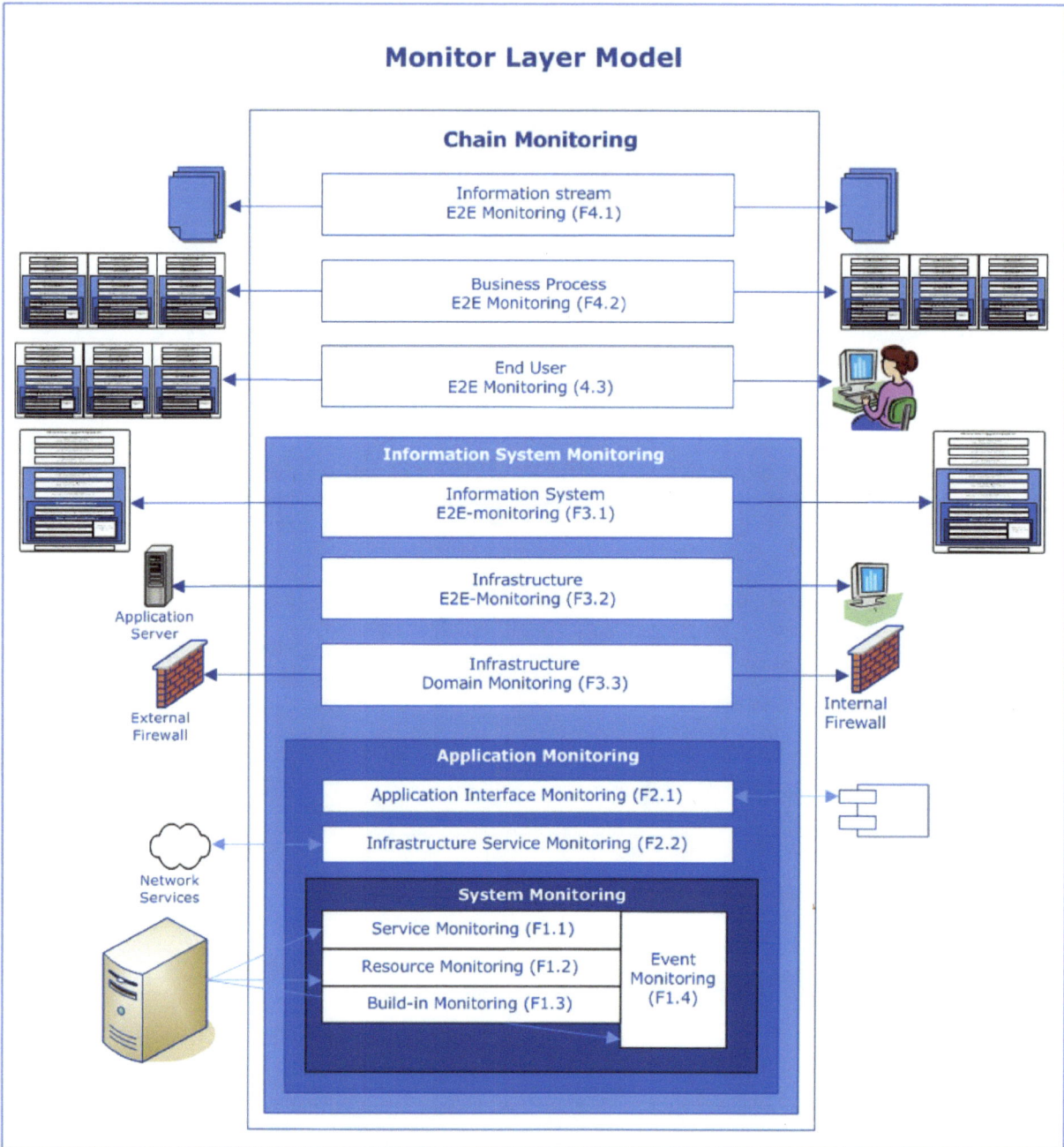

Figure 10-1, Monitor layer model - source: [Best 2015b].

FID	Name		Description
F1	**System Monitoring**		**The system monitor function focuses purely on one platform, such as an RS / 6000, web server, application server or router.**
	F1.1	Service monitoring	The monitoring of both infrastructure services and application services. The services are measured with a service management protocol, usually a Simple Network Management Protocol (SNMP) get.
	F1.2	Resource monitoring	Monitoring a single component on resource behaviour such as CPU, memory and network bandwidth.

FID	Name		Description
	F1.3	Built-in monitoring	An in-built monitoring is a monitor facility built into a product. This monitor function is read through an interface to obtain administrative information about the product.
	F1.4	Event monitoring	Event Monitoring includes all infrastructure components and infrastructure services as well as application events. The events can usually be read from local log files such as the application log, security log and error log. Many infrastructure services also write their events here.
F2	**Application monitoring**		**Unlike system monitoring focused on one platform, which does not use the platform's resources, application monitoring is aimed precisely at the interface of a platform and its environment.**
	F2.1	Application interface monitoring	The application interface monitor is specifically intended for application administrators so that they can at one glance determine that an application is "healthy". To this end, it is necessary that an application identifies which infrastructure components, infrastructure services and application services are of interest. In addition, measurements are made at the application level, which verifies the interaction between the infrastructure and the application code.
	F2.2	Infrastructure service monitoring	If an infrastructure service is "live", this does not mean that it also works well or even approachable. In order to establish this too, a dynamic test can be done at the infrastructure level where the service is called.
F3	**Information system monitoring**		**Information system monitoring is aimed at monitoring of an entire infrastructure domain or entire information system. An information system may consist of more applications.**
	F3.1	Information system E2E monitoring	The availability of an application does not yet mean that the user can work. Often applications are linked to complete chains (information systems).
	F3.2	Infrastructure E2E monitoring	The E2E monitoring infrastructure includes measuring the entire infrastructure layer. This monitoring is often used in the case of Wide Area Network (WAN).
	F3.3	Infrastructure domain monitoring	In case there are more cloud service providers or the network is divided into physically / logically separated domains, it is often desirable to monitor these domains separately in terms of availability, et cetera. There may also be other standards for these domains such as the DeMilitarized Zone (DMZ) domain versus the office automation network.
F4	**Chain monitoring**		**Chain monitoring is aimed at monitoring a chain from a user perspective, namely a business process, information flow or user transaction.**
	F4.1	Information Stream E2E monitoring	This is the measurement of a chain based on the information that is communicated and transformed.

FID	Name		Description
	F4.2	Business process monitoring	This concerns the monitoring of the entire business process based on the stated business process goals.
	F4.3	End user E2E monitoring	This involves measuring service norms based on individual users.

Table 10-1, Monitor functions.

Several monitor products have been marketed today. Of these, five variants are discussed in this chapter:
- Service desk monitoring;
- Built-in monitoring;
- Component based monitoring;
- End User eXperience Monitoring (EUX);
- Real User Monitoring (RUM).

In Table 10-2, a brief description per variation is included with reference to the monitor functions as defined in Table 10-1.

Product group	Short description	Monitor function
Service desk monitoring	The user himself is the monitor tool and the service desk is the registration tool.	-
Built-in monitoring	The application, which forms the basis for the ICT service, incorporates measurement functionality.	F1.3
Component based monitoring	Monitoring the ICT service based on the underlying infrastructure and application components.	F1.1, F1.2 and F1.4
EUX	Monitoring based on user simulation.	F3.1
RUM	Monitoring based on the actual use of the ICT service.	F4.3

Table 10-2, Product groups.

The following sections explain each variant, including a set of pros and cons. In order to give an impression of the versatility of measuring instruments, each variant identifies a number of tools and explains some specific features of a tool.

10.2 Service desk monitoring

The simplest and oldest way to measure service norms is to wait for a call from one or more users contacting the service desk. The tools used in this monitoring are the many service tools that have been launched on the market over the past few decades. These service tools can usually be classified into three classes, namely low-end, mid-end and high-end. The low-end tools are relatively cheap. By default, these tools provide limited functionality and are limited to customization. By default, the mid-end tools offer much more functionality and are also easier to customize than the low-end tools. However, these tools are significantly more expensive. The high-end service desk tools offer a lot of functionality by default and are also very easy to customize.

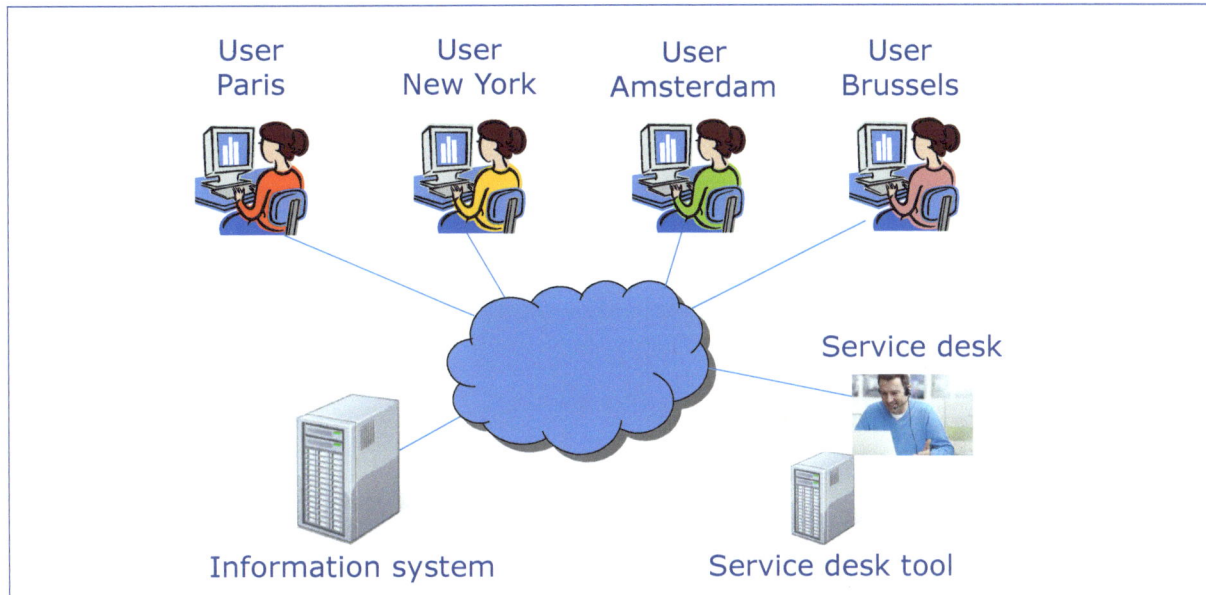

Figure 10-2, Service desk monitor architecture – source: [ITINFRA 2010-3].

10.2.1 Measure information
Examples of objects to be measured are:
- ICT services;
- ICT products;
- service management processes.

Examples of measurements are:
- lead times of incident, problems and change requests;
- request information;
- complaints;
- customer satisfaction.

10.2.2 Products
Frequently used tools include Topdesk, BMC Remedy Service Desk, CA Unicenter AHD, Support Magic Help Desk, HP Openview Service Desk, and more. The functionality of these tools has been further expanded over the years. Still, there are still differences in functionality to perceive. An example of a comprehensive service desk tool is CA Unicenter AHD. In addition to standard ITIL process support, this tool also provides workflow management. This allows the service management tasks to be defined around a product to be managed in the service management tool, such as handling standard changes.

10.2.3 Pros and cons
The benefits of this monitoring method are:
- The measurement is reasonably cheap because a form of service desk has often been set up.
- The measurement can be started immediately, even if only by keeping the notifications in a spreadsheet.
- The measurement originates from the user and, to some extent, is representative of what the user experiences.
- In addition to service norms such as availability and performance, service norms are also measured as delivery times of services and products.
- The measurement is reliable for as far as that it is recognizable to the user organization.

Disadvantages of this monitoring method are:
- The measurement allows only reactive service management.
- The question is how long the ICT service is already unavailable before the users call.

- It is often unclear what the extent of the disturbance is. How should it be reported?
- User notifications are highly subjective. What is a bad performance for example?
- Reporting on incidents contains inaccuracies such as double counts, impure detection and resolution times.

10.2.4 Cloud SLA Considerations
- Directly (call) to cloud service provider and ask for a service information portal.
- Use the cloud service provider's service desk tool.
- Automatic links between the service package of the own service organization and that of the cloud service provider so that:
  - incidents immediately visible to the cloud service provider;
  - the cloud service provider incidents can log in to the customer service desk.
- In heterogeneous disturbances, cloud service provider information is often required. This should allow the cloud service provider. It is also advisable to include this in the SLA.
- Take a SaaS service desk solution.

10.3 Built-in monitoring
During the construction of an application, the measurement functionality can be taken quite simply by determining measurement points that make the services offered measurable. This measurement functionality must be realized on the basis of user and management organization requirements. Also, this type of monitoring is already quite old. Examples include tracking counts in a complex cross-platform batch processing and lead times of messages by a chain. There are also providers who provide built-in monitoring facilities in the Common Of The Shelf (COTS) applications. The measurement data can be unlocked so that it can be passed on to its own monitor facility.

10.3.1 Measurement information
Examples of objects to be measured are:
- custom software;
- application interfaces.

Examples of measurements are:
- processing time of a transaction;
- response time from a request to another application.

10.3.2 Products
Examples of COTS products that have this built-in monitor feature for example Peoplesoft and Siebel.

10.3.3 Pros and cons
The benefits of this monitoring method are:
- The application can measure internal performance at various points, which is not visible with monitor tools outside of the application.
- The measurements can be logged including useful analysis information about the cause of the disturbance.
- The cost of these measurements is quite low. With custom-made applications, functionality has already been included in the design from the start.
- The measurements enable proactive management because trends are measurable.
- The detection time of disturbances is short, which increases availability.
- The measurement shows the location of the disturbance.

The disadvantages of this monitoring method are:
- The solution applies only to customized applications, unless the purchased application provides for this.
- The measurements must be included in all applications.
- The measurement only includes the transactions that are visible in the application. If users cannot use the application at all, this will not be detected.
- Changes to the measurement functionality means an adaptation to the application.

- The monitor function is intrusive, this means that the execution is at the expense of the resources assigned to the application.
- The monitor facility is internally oriented, it is not possible to monitor the performance of linked information systems. This also applies to infrastructure services such as network, storage and identity management.

10.3.4 Cloud SLA Considerations
- A built-in monitoring, such as that of Peoplesoft, must be connected to the cloud service provider's monitor. This must be agreed in the SLA.
- Built-in monitoring says something about the behaviour of the application. The customer must then be provided with the information online.
- Specific built-in monitoring can only be interpreted by the cloud service provider. This is where agreements must be made.

10.4 Component based monitoring

An ICT service can be decomposed in infrastructure and application components. For example, using IBM Component Failure Impact Analysis (CFIA) as described in ITIL. The sum of these components determines the quality of the ICT service. The SLA norms of an ICT service can thus be measured on the basis of these components. Figure 10-3 shows a sketch of this monitor architecture.

The monitor server collects the status information of the infrastructure and application components. This status information is varied and includes things like: Events written in log files, resource attachments of the infrastructure components, accessibility (reachability), availability and performance of services, set parameters, and general configuration information. This information can be collected by means of a push or a pull function. In a push action, active agents on a server are used to pass on the status of the affected components. In a pull operation, the monitor server itself collects the status of all components by walking it periodically.

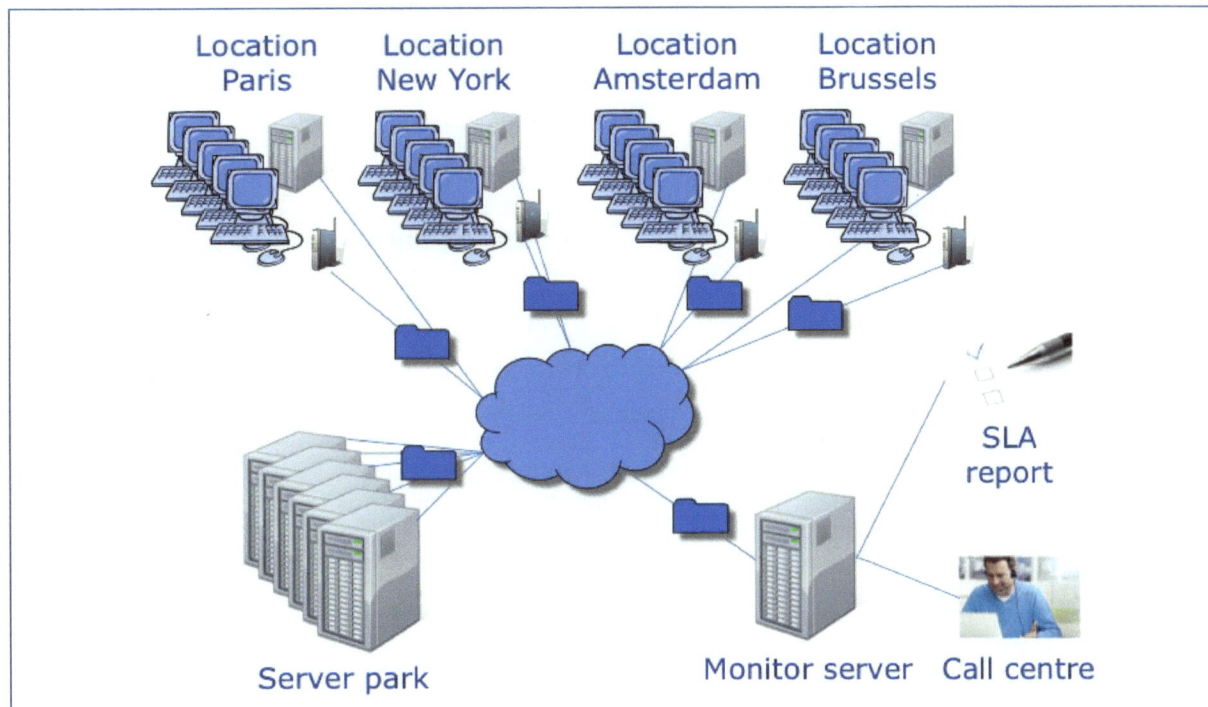

Figure 10-3, Component based monitor architecture – source: [ITINFRA 2010-3].

A best practice frequency to collect information from all components is once in fifteen minutes. Based on the centrally gathered information of the components, the monitor server determines what action to take. Periodically, a SLA report can be created about the results.

Of course, the redundancy of components and the like will be taken into account. If a duplicate component is unavailable, this service will still be available to the user.

10.4.1 Measure information
Service monitoring (F1.1):
- examples of objects to be measured are:
    - computer space, operating system, database management system and application;
- examples of measurements are:
    - dust, moisture, temperature, network services, communication services, platform services, storage services and application services;
- examples of measurement protocol are:
    - SNMP and service check.

Resource monitoring (F1.2):
- examples of objects to be measured are:
    - firewall, shaper, load balancer, SSL off loader, Wintel platform, Unix platform, Voice Response System (VRS), Voice Over IP (VOIP), Router, Switch and Storage Area Network (SAN);
- example of measurements are:
    - host alive, CPU load, RAM utilization, RAM swap space, disk I / O, NIC utilization and NIC broadcast;
- example measurement protocols are:
    - SNMP get, Remote Procedure Call (RPC) and SSH.

Event Monitoring (F1.4):
- examples of objects to be measured are:
    - log files of resource objects;
    - log files of service objects;
- examples of measurements are:
    - events;
- examples of measurement protocols are:
    - SNMP and retrieve log files.

10.4.2 Products
There are several vendors of tools on the market that partially or completely deliver this monitor architecture. Examples of commercial products include BMC Patrol, IBM Tivoli Monitoring, HP Operations Manager and CA Unicenter TNG. Examples of open source products are Zabbix and Munin. It is important to distinguish between (best-of-breed) umbrella solutions and integrated solutions. For example, SPS provides the Gensys comprehensive business service management solution in the form of an integrated tool that offers a wide range of features for a wide range of products. There are also vendors offering umbrella solutions by consolidating information from various tools, which each measure a segment of products, into one central monitor server.

10.4.3 Pros and cons
The benefits of this monitoring method are:
- In many cases, the measurement accurately reflects which location and component of the infrastructure or application is disturbed. Depending on the chosen tool, this requires little or much configuration effort.
- The registration of the measurement may include which management party must address the incident.
- The measurement provides insight into the availability, capacity, performance and security of the installed components.
- The total and available capacity of the infrastructure is well monitored based on current consumption. Trend analysis also forecasts future consumption in support of the capacity management process (proactive problem management).
- The consolidation allows events to be filtered out. For example, events involving the same disturbance may be bundled.

- The monitoring gives a disturbance of which business process / ICT service has been affected, provided that the relationships within the CMDB are well built. This can be responded quickly and adequately within the SLA agreements.
- The measurements and reports are performed without any human action being taken. Regarding auditing and / or verification with the service desk registration, this is very important.

The disadvantages of this monitoring method are:
- Depending on the chosen tool and the way it is set up, not all events (events) are monitored because they are too many. By setting filters, important events cannot be communicated to the administrators because they do not come through the set filters.
- If various tools are used that should outline the overall image, there are several factors that can cause events to be lost. Examples include the connectivity between the tools, the passing of events with a wrong message format, differences in performance indicator definition, et cetera.
- Measuring an ICT service based on the identified components always has the risk that components are missed and that the sum of the measurements differs from the end user experience.
- The measurement is aimed at the components, which does not say anything about the performance of a business transaction within the ICT service.
- The components that are deployed by more services can give an unclear picture of the resource usage of a service.
- The pull method may involve performance loss. The push method requires the management of agents on the objects to measure.

10.4.4 Cloud SLA considerations
- The cloud service provider must perform this form of monitoring itself. The degree of coverage in which the cloud service provider does this depends on the SLA, the knowledge and expertise of the cloud service provider and the cost price.
- By definition, the cloud service provider will try to handle the 80/20 rule. The question is what risks are controlled by adequate monitoring facilities.
- Requires every P1 incident a monitor gap analysis.
- Requirement of each E2E disturbance a declaration of failure per component and the check whether this was demonstrated by component monitoring.
- For heterogeneous incidents, the customer must have online access to that information online.

10.5 End User Experience monitoring (EUX)

In addition to the component-based monitor solution, there are also solutions that measure ICT services E2E. In practice, there are two mainstreams to be distinguished, the EUX and the RUM. The difference between both is that the EUX solution measures the ICT service based on a user simulation, while the RUM solution measures the actual transactions of the users. Following is an explanation of the EUX solution, after which the RUM solution is discussed.

The EUX solution is based on a user simulation. This simulation takes place by the actual use of the application by recording a user with a recorder and periodically playing the resulting scripts (synthetic transactions). To this end, one or more PCs (robots) are used that are set up in a closed space.

Most vendors provide a solution that manages the scripts on a central server. New or custom scripts are distributed by the central server to the robots. The scheduling of the scripts to be scrubbed by robots is also centrally arranged. The results of the robot measurements are collected centrally and compared to the service norms. In case of a violation, an alert will be issued.

The decision whether or not a service norm has been exceeded is governed by rules such as: "If seventy percent of the XYZ transaction robots detect an elapsed time of more than three seconds, then an alert must be issued with a severity critical." Figure 10-4 Shows an example of an EUX implementation.

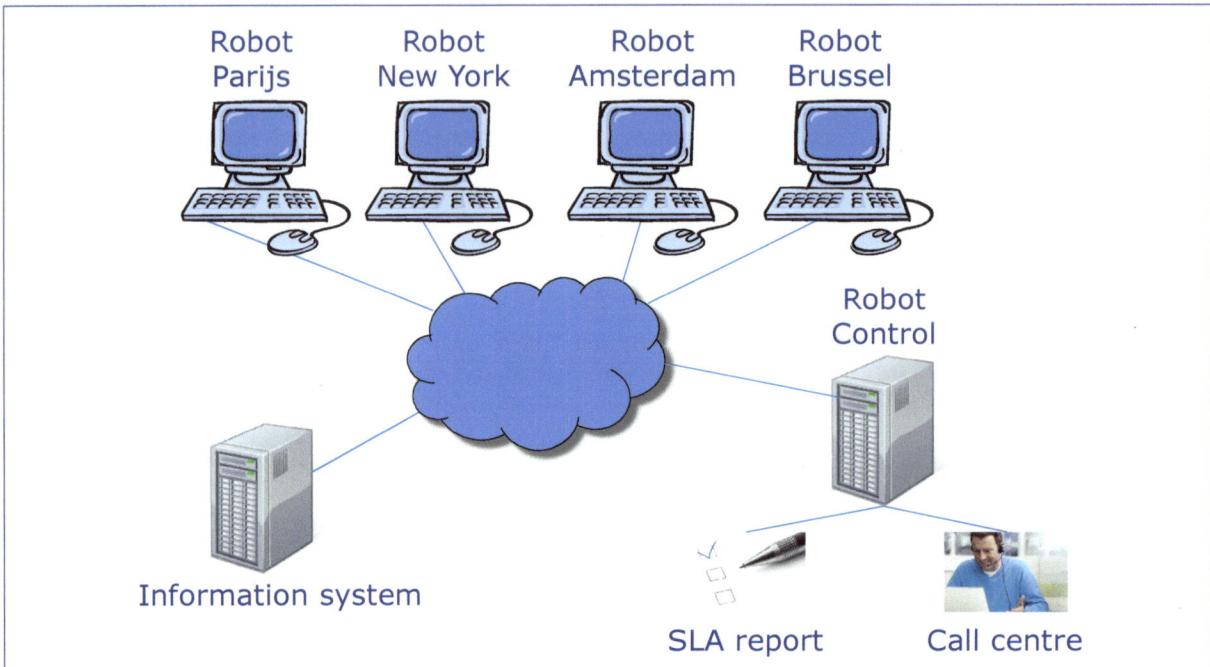

Figure 10-4, EUX-monitor architecture – source: [IT INFRA 2010-3].

10.5.1 Products

There are various products on the market with totally different functionality, quality and pricing, such as Compuware (Client Vantage), Oracle (Enterprise Manager) and HP (Business Activity Centre). An example of extensive EUX functionality is Gomez's tooling acquired by Compuware in November 2009. This solution is offered as a SaaS, which measures active agents (robots) from a cloud application. This EUX solution is standard integrated with the Compuware RUM solution offered. As a result, disturbances from the simulation can be compared with the actual use of the ICT service.

There are also cloud service providers offering SaaS solutions for Internet applications. The Internet ICT service from various locations in the world or the Netherlands is measured, alerted and reported. Usually, the cost is a few tens of euros per transaction per month. There are also freeware tools like Nagios in the market. These tools also enable user transactions to be simulated. Important additional facilities are the back-tracing of the cause of a disturbance. This can be done by the robot itself by means of additional measurements and analyses as well as links with other tools that provide additional information and analyses.

10.5.2 Pros and cons

The benefits of this monitoring method are:
- The measurement comes close to what the user experiences.
- The measurement does not require knowledge of the various components underlying the service.
- The measurement provides a good indication of all disturbances that could be visible to the user in the overall service regardless of the nature (infrastructure, application or workload).
- The SaaS measurements do not require the implementation of monitoring software and can be used quickly.

The disadvantages of this monitoring method are:
- The observation of the robots is limited to a number of points in time, from a limited number of locations, with a limited number of functions and with a limited set of data.
- The measurement provides limited information about the location of the disturbance (backtracking).

- The robot influences the system to be monitored. So, it is important to look at the resource (memory, disk capacity, et cetera) and pollution of the production databases by the monitoring tool.
- The robot must have an account with a password that does not change. Anyone who knows the account and password has the same rights as the robot.
- When servicing the application, check that the robot is still working. Certain adjustments to the user interface of the application are disastrous for the correct operation of the robot.

10.5.3 Cloud SLA considerations

D-03

- Do not allow EUX monitoring by the cloud service provider, but preferably by a cloud service broker in connection with objectivity.
- The advantage of investing the EUX monitor facility with the cloud service provider is the exploitation of EUX backtrack functionality.
- The EUX monitor provider is a user who requires security. This must also be agreed upon with the cloud service provider.
- Look out for mutations done by the EUX monitor facility. If this facility is not provided by the SaaS cloud service provider itself, it can void the support contract.

10.6 Real User Monitoring (RUM)

A recent development is to monitor the actual use of ICT service without affecting the ICT service (non-intrusive). This technology measures the network traffic that is the basis of the ICT service that is the performance that is being delivered. To this end, the network traffic packages are copied and analysed on a monitor server. Figure 10-5 shows an example of a RUM monitor architecture.

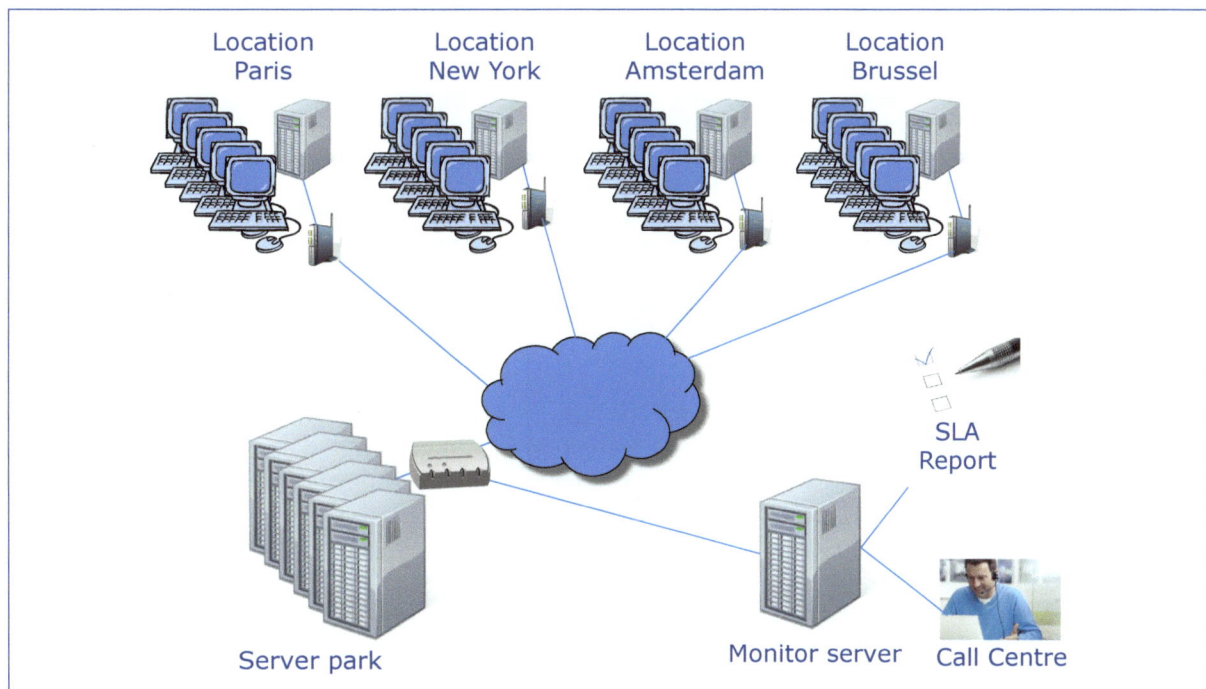

Figure 10-5, RUM-monitor architecture – source: [ITINFRA 2010-3].

10.6.1 Products

There are a limited number of vendors on the market that have met the measurement of service norms based on a Network Protocol Analysis (NPA). Examples of these tools include: HP (HP Real User Monitor), Compuware (ClientVantage Agentless Monitoring), and Oracle (Real User Experience Insight (RUEI)). The interesting thing about the last-mentioned solution is that these three important RUM features are integrated. Thus, the measured user transactions can be played back. Indeed, with a RUM solution, all (HTML) transaction traffic is analysed and logged.

There is also a business intelligence feature that not only measures the availability and performance, but also the user's navigation behaviour, page load time, inventory, and so forth. The third function is the root-cause analyses that can be analysed which part of the application, the causes the disturbance.

10.6.2 Pros and cons
Advantages of this monitoring method are:
- The measurement is non-intrusive, the monitoring does not affect the measurement and does not use resources assigned to the application.
- The measurement is based on actual transactions, not on simulations or samples. This makes the measurement objective and reliable.
- The measurement gives insight into the actual behaviour of the information system.
- Changed applications are also automatically measured. No scripts need to be modified. Each real user action is measured.
- Not only norms such as availability and performance are good measurable, but also the behaviour of the user. For example, the navigation behaviour of users in a web application can be determined. Based on this, marketing analyses can be conducted.

Disadvantages of this monitoring method are:
- The network packages must contain enough information to be able to correlate with the ICT service. This can be done by adding tags to a HTML request and based on a URL structure.
- Often, these solutions are highly dependent on the submitted protocol (HTTP / HTTPS). As a result, only web-based applications can be monitored.
- Changes to the application must be assessed on impact. In most cases, all data is still measured. However, alert rules and reports need to be reviewed.
- The measurements contain production data that can be very confidential. Measures must be taken to secure it. Most tools provide for this.
- The location of the cause of a disturbance cannot be determined. However, many vendors offer solutions to link the RUM monitor functionality to analysis tooling.
- Recognizing the business transactions in the network packages and possibly adjusting the application to measure these transactions can take the necessary time. This also depends on the complexity of the business service.
- The enormous ability of this tooling has a big brother-watching-you side effect. Good agreements must be made with the users of the information system.
- The measurements are only useful if there is a baseline of good performance. In an organization with fifty applications each having twenty to thirty different types of transactions, such a baseline is very difficult to determine.

10.6.3 Cloud SLA considerations
D-04
- Do not allow the RUM monitor to be performed by the cloud service provider, but preferably by a cloud service broker in connection with objectivity.
- The RUM monitor may store more data than the customer knows. Watch out for this data storage in relation to the laws and regulations.

10.7 Do's en Don'ts
For the effective and efficient setup of an ICT service monitoring, the following recommend-dations apply:
- Define upfront clear constraints for the monitor proviosining.
- To be able to switch quickly, an E2E monitoring of an ICT service must always be supplemented with a component measurement or built-in measurement that can determine the cause of the service norm deviation. There are several suppliers offering different integrated solutions. When selecting tooling, take note of what is possible. If integration is limited, particular attention should be paid to the integrating possibilities.
- Apply a norm for the maximum impact of the monitor provisioning on the ICT service. A widely-used norm here is five percent. This norm must then be monitored again.
- Consider the monitor function as part of the ICT service whose norm is measured. In case of a change, the impact on the monitor facility must be taken.

- During the acceptance of the ICT service, handle the monitor facility to measure the SLA norm in the acceptance environment.
- Perform trend analyses as a means of preventing incidents.
- Determine whether a defect detected by an EUX or RUM is measured by component based monitoring. In this case, handle the control matrix as shown in Table 10-1.
- Realizing that setting up a good monitor facility often costs a lot of time and money. This investment is only recovered if the resulting monitoring facility is actually used and the management gives control to the service management organization based on the results. A preliminary investigation to determine what the ambition level is at the workplace and in management is an important starting point.

Monitor matrix	Component based monitoring OK	Component based monitoring Not OK
RUM / EUX OK	The service norms are met.	The user is not affected by the disturbance. Verify that this is due to redundancy or error in E2E monitoring.
RUM / EUX Not OK	The user is experiencing the disturbance. Verify that this disturbance should have been measured by the current component based monitor functionality and whether it can still be measured.	The service norms are not met. Determine which measures need to be taken to get them.

Table 10-3, Control matrix – source: [ITINFRA 2010-4].

It should be avoided that:
- the measurement is not focused on the quality objective of the business processes;
- the measurement does not respond to the SLA norms;
- the translation of the technical norm to business norm is not possible;
- there are too many measurements to be able to process;
- the measurements are unreliable.

10.8 Conclusion

Each monitor architecture has pros and cons. There will always be a combination of monitoring tools necessary for the proper monitoring of an ICT service. Ideally, the service norms E2E are measured with an EUX and / or RUM solution, so the measurement is as close as possible to what the user experiences. With only a device of an EUX and / or RUM solution cannot be sufficient. There will always be a component-based solution for locating a disturbance. In addition, both solutions enhance each other, as shown in the control matrix (Table 10-3).

P-09

Table 10-5 gives an overview of some of the advantages and disadvantages mentioned in this section, supplemented by a number of additional points. Table 10-5 indicates only a certain functionality of a monitor solution. There are always ifs or buts to name when completing Table 10-5.

It must also be said that tools do not fit always pure within one class of a monitor solution. Nevertheless, the table gives a nice indication of the possibilities and impossibilities of the chosen solution. Each restriction listed in the table is worth at least one check of the chosen solution.

In order to better compare the various solutions, Table 10-4 gives an overview of some characteristic measurements per solution.

Monitor solution	Characteristic measurements
Service desk	Incidents and changes.
Built-in	Number of transactions, turnaround transactions, errors per application module.
Component based	Derived availability and performance of the ICT service based on component disturbance. Resource measurements are performed such as CPU load, memory consumption, network bandwidth usage. Further event measurements such as MS Windows logs, Z/OS, Linux et cetera. And finally, service measurements such as Apache web servers, MS IIS, print services et cetera.
EUX	Availability and performance of synthetic transactions of application functions. The measurements relate to lead time and availability (HTTP status codes et cetera.).
RUM	Availability, performance of business transactions. The measurements include lead time, availability, web page load time, navigation behaviour (click paths), sales articles, error message and so on.

Table 10-4, Characteristic measurements.

	Service desk	Built-in	Component Based	EUX	RUM
Measurement range service norms:					
- Availability	green	green	green	green	green
- Performance	green	green	green	green	green
- Capacity	orange	orange	green	orange	orange
- Security	yellow	orange	green	orange	orange
- Navigation behaviour	orange	orange	green	orange	green
Special measurement functionality:					
- Automatic detection	orange	green	green	green	green
- Detection without users	orange	green	green	green	orange
- Proactive management	orange	green	green	orange	orange
(Trend analysis)	orange	green	green	orange	green *
- Measurement of infrastructure log error messages	orange	green	green	orange	orange
- Measurement application log	yellow	green	orange	yellow	green
Measurement information:					
- Location of the disturbance	yellow	yellow	green	orange	yellow **
- Related components	yellow	yellow	green	orange	orange
- Indication solution group	yellow	yellow	green	orange	orange
Measurement range:					
- Infrastructure components	yellow	orange	green	orange	orange
- Application components	yellow	green	green	orange	light green ***
- Business transactions	yellow	green	orange	orange	green
Measurement limitation by:					
- Measurement frequency	orange	orange	light green	light green	orange
- Measurement locations	orange	orange	orange	green	orange

	Service desk	Built-in	Com-ponent Based	EUX	RUM
- Measurement functionality	No	No	Yes	Yes	No
Measuring influence:					
- Databases remain untouched	Yes	Yes	Yes	No	Yes
- Non-intrusive	Yes	No	No	No	Yes
Maintenance:					
Adaptability	Yes	Partly	Yes	Yes	Yes
Sensitive to application adjustments	Yes	Yes	Yes	No	****

Legend: | Yes | Partly | Limited | No |

*) This is possible by the use of additional tools that may or may not be offered as an integrated solution.

**) RUM can locate the disruption to client, server, or network areas.

***) Those application components that can be viewed from the user interface are, however, non-derivative internal components of network traffic.

****) Application changes are transparent to the monitoring tools in the current generation of space tools, as applications are recognized based on URL structures. Any necessary tags for recognizing transactions can be added from a Content Management System (CMS).

Table 10-5, Pros and cons per monitor solution - source: [ITINFRA 2010-3].

10.9 Summary

Monitoring of service norms has been highly developed over the years. There have been several monitor architectures that are very useful to support the service level manager when monitoring the service norms. It is therefore important that the service level manager understands the possibilities of the monitor architectures and which things are not possible.

It is especially important for the service level manager to understand what aspects may or may not be measurable when handling a particular monitor architecture. As a result, he can properly assess the unreliability of the SLA reports.

11 Cloud changes and projects

Message:
- Changes and projects are alterations to solutions that can bring along risks. These must be controlled.
- The acceptance of cloud service changes and projects should be risk-based. The best way to do this is to use an architecture approach.

Reading guideline:
Paragraph 11.1 describes the GSA-7 step approach to control the risks of changes and projects related to cloud services. In paragraph 11.2 the conclusion has been described.

11.1 GSA 7-step approach

The Generic & Specific Acceptance Criteria (GSA) 7-step approach is pictured in Figure 11-1. The grey blocks in the left column reflect the relationship with the service level management process. The grey blocks in the right column show the relationship with project management and the change management process. This GSA 7-step approach is intended to control the risks that entail changes. These steps can be used to control risks of alterations to cloud services.

Step 1. Image

The first step is to map the landscapes in which the change takes place, namely the business processes, applications involved and interfaces and the infrastructure landscape. In the case of an IaaS and PaaS, the latter landscape map focuses mainly on the interfaces between the IaaS / PaaS service and its own infrastructure. In case of a SaaS, both the application landscape map and the infrastructure map will be focussed at the interface with the cloud service provider.

Step 2. Building blocks

The second step is to divide the Landscape Maps into building blocks, called System Building Blocks (SBBs). These building blocks are built from service layers containing the functional building blocks. Each change and project determines which building blocks contain new or adjusted products. This is the basis for the impact assessment of the change of the project. Building blocks with new products are red-coloured, building blocks with modified products yellow and building blocks used only green. Unused building blocks are greyed out. In case of an IaaS or PaaS, one or more service layers of the infrastructure can be declared completely out of scope because they are out of the customer's field of view. For a SaaS, this also applies to one or more layers of application building blocks (application services).

Important to recognize is that building blocks or layers of building blocks can thus be hit without the customer being able to assess whether there are any risks involved. This is the essence of the question whether cloud SLAs are reliable. Unrecognized or uncontrolled risks are often the cause of SLA norm deviations. In case of a private cloud solution, impact analysis can be performed with the cloud service provider. In case of a public cloud solution this will usually not be the case.

Step 3. Risk assessment

The risk assessment is done by brainstorming one hour with each of the specialists involved in each aspect area (business process, application and infrastructure). Usually five employees are involved. In any case, an architect, administrator, tester and developer. Perhaps the customer (employee business process) and / or cloud service provider may also be involved in the risk session.

The building blocks that are greyed out in the impact analysis are disregarded in the risk assessment. Most of the time is spent on the building blocks that are red-coloured in the impact analysis and then the building blocks that are yellow-coloured. The green building blocks do not generally give rise to risks, at most risks such as building blocks, for example by the number of competitors. Any risk is determined by the countermeasure and an owner is granted.

For the building blocks that are included in the cloud service of the cloud service provider, the risks can be looked at on the basis of general terms. The building blocks are not yet determined in step two let alone the impact of the change / project on the products within these building blocks. Nevertheless, the identified risks on the main features are also an opportunity to go through the follow-up steps of the GSA 7-step approach. The countermeasures of these risks are important aspects of naming and concluding the contract or the SLA.

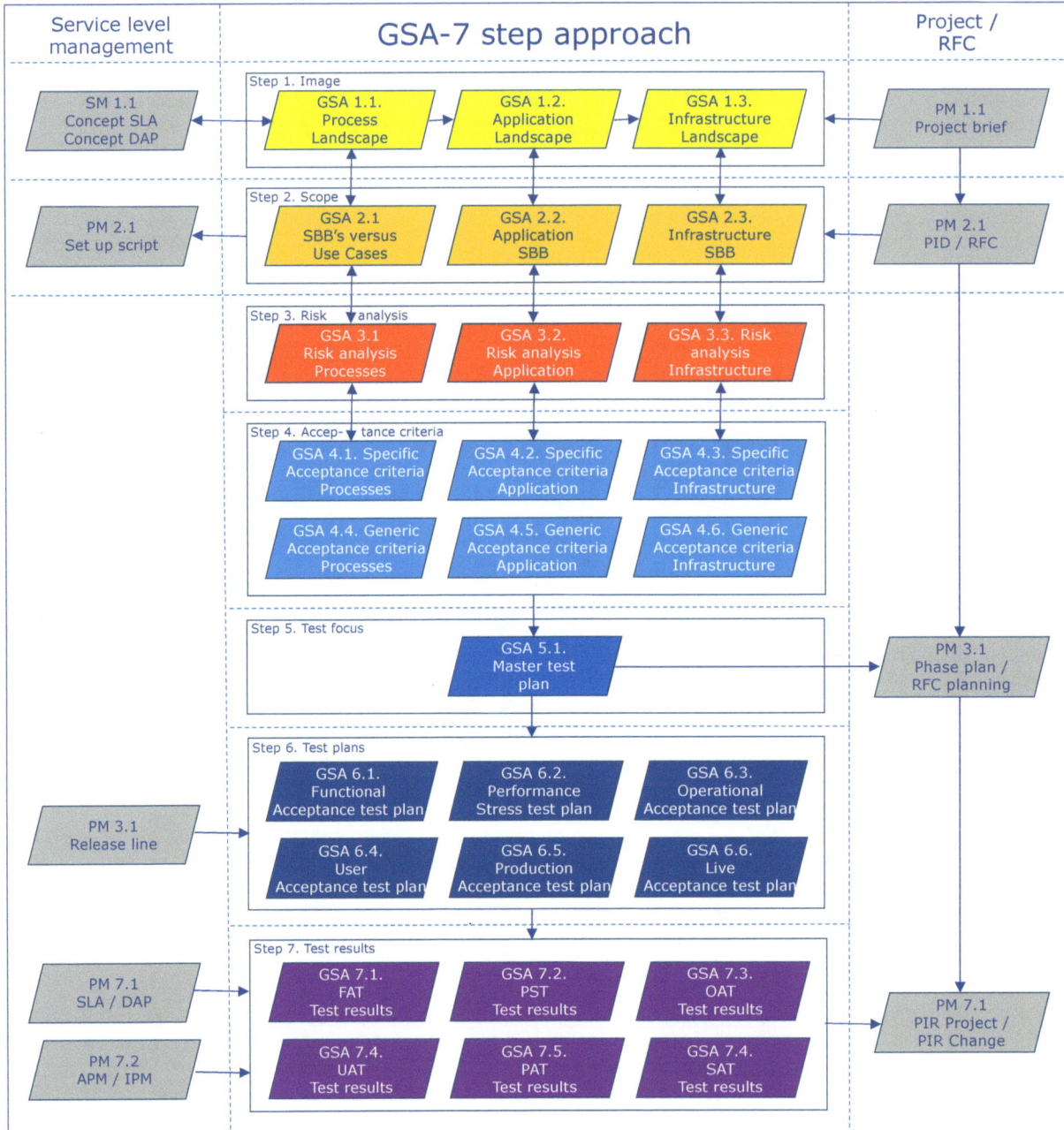

Figure 11-1, GSA 7-step approach – source: [BEST 2014a].

Step 4. Acceptance criteria

For each countermeasure of risk, a review of compliance with the countermeasure is determined. This review is performed upon acceptance of the service. These reviews are specifically called acceptance criteria because they are unique to an information system. In addition, there are generic risks, with generic countermeasures which are therefore called generic acceptance criteria. These generic acceptance criteria are selected for applicability for the change / project.

For the building blocks supported by the cloud service provider, acceptance criteria can also be set. These can be included in the contract.

Step 5. Master test plan
The acceptance criteria must be determined in which acceptance tests they are conducted and which should be given the most time. This timing is based on the probability (high / medium / low) and the impact (large / medium / small) of the risk. Thus, the particular risks form the test strategy. Hereby, the risks that are accepted by the customer are an exception. These are not tested or tested. Whether the cloud service provider cooperates with a master test plan depends on the relationship. Especially with a private solution, this will be the case.

Step 6. Test plans
The test plans must be prepared so that they can be executed. Testing techniques may be used as described by Test Management APproach Next (TMap Next). Creating test plans for a cloud service is possible for a private solution. For a public solution, a suitcase can be chosen based on a black box approach. However, this must be reported to the cloud service provider because unexpected effects can occur which the cloud service provider sees the customer as an attacker. Another possibility is to include the test cases in an audit or by viewing in the Third-Party Memorandum (TPM) that the cloud service provider issues or the identified risks are governed by the statement of a TPA.

Step 7. Test results
The test results indicate whether the risks are controlled. This is of course limited to those test plans that could be carried out.

11.2 Conclusion
Because cloud services are characterized by the closed character, the determination of risks is not always possible. As the customer manages more functionality, the possibility of risk management is stronger. On the other hand, the cloud service provider generally wants to safeguard a lot of risks in order not to get out of the market. A customer of a cloud service can in any case test all services from a black box approach based on identified risks. This should take into account unexpected effects. The cloud service provider must therefore be informed of such tests. However, testing may be unnecessary if, on the basis of a TPM, it can be determined that certain risks are controlled. In the cloud, SLA (and DAP) the degree of risk management must be recorded. In particular, the cooperation of the cloud service provider and the provision of information is of great importance. If this does not happen, the customer implicitly takes many risks without even recognizing it.

12 Cloud support en maintenance

Message:
- The support of cloud services requires determining the interfaces of service management processes between those of the customer and the cloud service provider.
- Risks can be determined and controlled by following the GSA 7-step approach.

Reading guideline:

Section 12.1 describes support aspects and section 12.2 the maintenance aspects of cloud services. These aspects must be included in the cloud SLAs.

12.1 Support aspects

T-10

The main tips for setting up a cloud SLA are:
- handle requirements per support process;
- classify these to procedures;
- Select all process requisitions performed by the cloud service provider (DAP demarcation plate);
- have these requirements audited in the TPA / TPM.

Support requirements

For each support process such as incident management, it is necessary to consider requirements that facilitate support for using the cloud services. For example, it is important to determine how an incident can be reported and whether there is online support for significant disturbances. These requirements will vary per cloud service. For a SaaS service, other requirements will apply to an IaaS service. There is also a difference between the requirements for private and public services. More about managing requirements per management process is published in the book Quality Control & Assurance [Best 2012].

Examples of incident management requirements are:
- incidents can be reported through an online service;
- of each incident, tracking and tracing is possible;
- the cloud service provider provides a search function for existing incidents and Frequently Asked Questions (FAQ).

Examples of problem management requirements are:
- the cloud service provider offers incidental workarounds within set SLA times;
- known errors have been published;
- the cloud service provider is involved in analysing problems where more parties are involved.

Examples of business information management requirements are:
- interface files are traceable in processing;
- the cloud service provider offers the possibility of manual correction of errors;
- the one-time processing of information is possible on request.

Classify to procedures

By classifying the requirements for procedures per process, it is possible to specify in the Cloud Service DAP exactly which interface arrangements are expected.

Selection

The quality of service is determined by matching who does what. The cloud Service provider will perform a number of things by default. It is important to determine what the customer does and what is expected of the cloud service provider. The delta between this expectation and the standard service is important for the selection of the cloud solution. Customized solutions for cloud solutions will be difficult, but with private solutions this may be the case.

Audit
The agreements made in the DAP must be checked in terms of operation. This can be done through a TPA / TPM.

12.2 Maintenance aspects
In the field of maintenance of a cloud service, a number of risk aspects should be considered:
- portfolio management;
- lifecycle management;
- Development-, Test-, Acceptance- and Production Environment (DTAP);
- Information security management.

Portfolio management
R7.1 The cloud service provider's portfolio differs from that of the customer in the future (SLA 5.5.2).

Portfolio management concerns the strategic levelling of the solutions used to provide information to the business processes for information systems, applications and infrastructure products. The cloud solutions are part of it. However, these solutions should continue to close to the portion of the portfolio that is not filled in as a cloud solution.

This can happen in two ways:
1. The cloud service provider is a strategic partner of the customer and agrees with the completion of the portfolio and agrees with the cloud solutions.
2. The customer chooses other cloud applications in case of changes in the portfolio between products that are in-house and provided by the cloud service provider and are not bridged.

In most cases, option two will be necessary. This also means that the cloud solutions require strong exit conditions so that redevelopment of cloud solutions can be easily, quickly and managed.

Lifecycle management
R7.2 Due to software obsolescence, the client runs security risks (SLA 5.5.3).
- For an individual product, attention must be paid to innovativeness. Obsolete products typically have lower service quality, such as security. This can be secured in a cloud SLA by an agreement such as the N-1 policy, which ensures that the applied products are not older than the most recent released version.

R7.3 Software release, versions and patches disrupt the application (SLA 5.2.2).
- At the operational level, it should be avoided that any changes to the software release, versions and patches are affected by service. This can be done by agreeing on a maintenance window. If this is not possible because a standard cloud SLA is offered, then the own organization must add to it.

DTAP
R7.4 Transition from acceptance to production is not regulated (DAP 4.2.23).
- Certainly, in case of an IaaS and PaaS, the cloud service provider will be able to offer different environments in a simple way. These should be linked. In case of a configurable SaaS solution, there must also be a form of a Development-, Test-, Acceptance-, Production environment (DTAP).

In the cloud service decline, DTAP facilities should not forget that the transition from the A environment to the P environment is easy and not too expensive.

R7.5 Unscheduled maintenance disrupts service (DAP attachment 2).
- The changes in the environments should be planned. Sometimes a change to an environment must be excluded. This must be included in the SLA. Possibly it is possible to take a double service to compensate for the loss of an environment. As in the case of lifecycle management, the customer will have to adapt to the given availability of the environments.

R7.6 The norms of the A environment are insufficient (rights, data encryption, data scrambling (SLA 3.4.10)?
- Finally, the DTAP service must take into account the service norms used in the A environment. If these norms in terms of rights, data encryption or data scrambling are insufficient to perform representative acceptance tests, this may lead to poor acceptance, which causes unnecessary problems in production.

Information security management
R7.7 Security incidents are accessible to all, measure: requires a separate process, separate handling (R4.2.25).
- An aspect that should not be underestimated is dealing with security incidents. If these incidents are accessible to unauthorized persons, there may be potential for service vulnerabilities to be a source of hacking and the like. Agreements on how to deal with security incidents should therefore be recorded in the cloud SLA and / or DAP. Preferably there is a separate security process or handling.

13 Cloud SLA check lists

13.1 Programme of requirements

Before starting a selection of cloud service providers, it is important to compose a Program of Requirements (PoR). This section gives an example of a program of requirements. When using this list, it is advisable to add two columns pinpoint the relevance and reason for each criterion.

#	Criteria	Form
Common		
CM-01	Service name	Text box
CM-02	Service description	Section
CM-03	Main category	Dropdown
CM-04	Subcategory	Dropdown
Target audience		
TA-01	Target group sole proprietorship	Yes / No
TA-02	Target group 2 - 10 employees	Yes / No
TA-03	Target group 10 - 49 employees	Yes / No
TA-04	Target group 50 - 250 employees	Yes / No
TA-05	Target group 250 - 1000 employees	Yes / No
TA-06	Target group Enterprise 1000+ employees	Yes / No
TA-07	Dutch language	Yes / No
TA-08	English language	Yes / No
TSA-09	Other languages	Section
Provider data		
PD-01	What is your formal organization name?	Text box
PD-02	What is the name of your contact person?	Text box
PD-03	[Other contact person]	[Other]
Market strategy		
MS-01	In what markets is the cloud service provider active?	Section
MS-02	In which markets is the focus?	Section
MS-03	What is the growth strategy?	Section
MS-04	What is the cloud service provider's market share in these markets?	Percentage
MS-05	At what market stage are the services of the cloud service provider?	Section
Business model		
BM-01	What is the cloud service provider's business model? How is the money being earned?	Section
BM-02	Does the cloud service provider have different business models?	Section
Innovation		
IN-01	What is the percentage of your budget used for innovation?	Section
IN-02	How often are new functionalities added to the portfolio?	Section
IN-03	Who are your primary competitors?	Section
IN-04	How big is the Research & Development (R&D) budget?	Section

#	Criteria	Form
IN-05	Geographical presence	Section
IN-06	Does the cloud service provider operate globally or is the provider targeting on a particular geographic area?	Section
IN-07	In which countries does the cloud service provider have physical offices?	Section
Financial health		
FH-01	What are the financial key figures of the company? Does the cloud service provider provide insight into its revenue, liquidity, solvency and repayment capacity)?	Section
Transparency		
OP-01	Is the cloud service provider a member of standardization organization such as Object Management Group (OMG) and Oasis9?	Yes / No
OP-02	Which standardization organization is cloud service provider member?	Section
OP-03	To what extent does the cloud service provider contribute to the development of open standards?	Section
OP-04	Which open standards does the cloud service provider have on its name?	Section
OP-05	Does the cloud service provider (parts) offer its solution as an open source?	Yes / No
OP-06	What parts does the cloud service provider make available and in what way?	Section
OP-07	Does the cloud service provider use open source products?	Yes / No
OP-08	Which open source products does the cloud service provider use?	Section
OP-09	Is the cloud service provider involved in open source initiatives?	Yes / No
OP-10	What open (-source) initiatives do the cloud service provider take?	Section
Organisation		
OR-01	What is the cloud service provider's date of establishment?	Date
OR-02	How many employees does the cloud service provider (approximate) employ?	Text box
OR-03	How much revenue does the cloud service provider (approximate) have?	Text box
OR-04	How does the cloud service provider ensure stability for its customers so that it continues in the contract periods?	Section
OR-05	What certifications does the cloud service provider have (ISO 20000, ISAE 3402)?	Section
OR-06	How has the certification been performed?	Section
OR-07	Does the cloud service provider have the available audit reports available on request?	Yes / No
OR-08	Where can these audits be requested?	Section
OR-09	Are there any fees for obtaining audits?	Yes / No
OR-10	Can the cloud service provider provide three credentials for this service?	Yes / No
OR-11	What are the three credentials?	Section
Disaster		
DS-01	Is the cloud service provider liable to data loss due to an emergency?	Yes / No
DS-02	What guarantees does the cloud service provider provide for backup and recovery?	Section
DS-03	How long is the recovery time to restore a backup?	Section
DS-04	At what level can data be recovered from a backup?	Section

#	Criteria	Form
DS-05	What are the costs of performing a backup?	Section
Data		
DA-01	Is the data physically stored in the Netherlands?	Yes / No
DA-02	Is the data physically stored in Europe?	Yes / No
DA-03	Does the data stay inside Europe? This includes backups, offline storage, and more.	Yes / No
DA-04	In which countries is the data stored?	Section
DA-05	Does the customer remain the intellectual owner of the data when using the service?	Yes / No
DA-06	Can the cloud service provider use the customer's data (for personal purposes)?	Yes / No
DA-07	If so, for what purposes does this apply?	Section
DA-08	Is there a strong guarantee that the cloud service provider cannot get access to the data?	Yes / No
DA-09	How was this (hard) warranty organized?	Section
DA-10	Who is responsible for the integrity and confidentiality of the data?	Section
DA-11	How is data transfer from the customer to the cloud service provider and vice versa encrypted?	Yes / No
DA-12	What form of encryption is applied with which key length?	Section
DA-13	Is the data stored at the cloud service provider also encrypted?	Yes / No
DA-14	To what extent is the cloud service provider liable for data loss due to an emergency?	
DA-15	Does the cloud service provider warrant that customer data is not shared with other customers?	Yes / No
DA-16	Does the cloud service provider warrant that the customer's data is saved as needed as long as necessary?	Yes / No
DA-17	Does the cloud service provider warrant that the customer's data is removed at the customer's request?	Yes / No
DA-18	Does the cloud service provider warrant that customers' data can be retrieved by the customer so that the customer can transfer this data to another place?	Yes / No
Functionality		
FU-01	Are the services of the cloud service provider public / private or hybrid?	Hybrid
FU-02	What are the connected networks (Internet and others)?	Internet
FU-03	Is API access possible?	Yes / No
FU-04	Is self-service provisioning possible (self-systems and / or users add and start)?	Yes / No
FU-05	What functionality is provided by the cloud service provider?	Section
FU-06	What functionality is optional?	Section
FU-07	How often are functional updates performed?	Section
FU-08	How to decide on new updates?	Section
FU-09	Are changes in functionality announced?	Yes / No
FU-10	What is the minimum period used for announcing changes?	Section
FU-11	Is backwards compatibility guaranteed?	Yes / No
FU-12	How soon can new users be created?	Section

#	Criteria	Form
FU-13	How fast is new functionality added? Does this also depend on the customer's desired functionality?	Section
FU-14	How fast are security patches implemented? How is this process implemented?	Section
In what way does the provider evolve its service?		
EV-01	Is there a roadmap available?	Yes / No
EV-02	Is the cloud service provider's roadmap public?	Yes / No
EV-03	Where is this roadmap (URL) available?	URL
EV-04	How far is the roadmap going?	text box
EV-05	To what extent does the organization have influence the roadmap?	Section
EV-07	Can an organization choose not to join new features?	Yes / No
EV-08	Can the organization choose to turn on or off beta functionality?	Yes / No
EV-09	Is there a user group?	Yes / No
EV-10	How was the user group organized?	Section
EV-11	Are the minutes public?	Yes / No
EV-12	What are the dependencies of the provider with the subcontractors?	Section
EV-13	What agreements has the cloud service provider made with its subcontractors?	Section
EV-14	How does the cloud service provider deal with identity management?	Section
EV-15	Is a connection to the organization's user directory possible?	Yes / No
EV-16	Which user directories are supported?	Section
EV-17	Is a connection to generic authentication facilities possible?	Yes / No
EV-18	Which generic authentication services are supported?	Section
EV-19	Does the cloud service provider support the current market practice (e.g. Security Assertion Markup Language (SAML) 2.0)?	Yes / No
Transition		
TR-01	Does the cloud service provider support migration to another provider?	Yes / No
TR-02	What standards and procedures does the cloud service provider support for data migration? What possibilities are there?	Section
TR-03	Can a configuration (e.g., the default sort order of email, used tags) be migrated to and from the cloud service provider?	Yes / No
Exit		
EX-01	How is a customer's exit supported?	Section
EX-02	What procedures does the cloud service provider apply at this point?	Section
EX-03	Will data be available after exit? In which manner? For how long?	Section
EX-04	Can the data be migrated to the organization (customer) or to another cloud service provider?	Yes / No
EX-05	How is this migration of data supported?	Section
EX-06	In what way does the cloud service provider ensure that the data incidental to the institution (including metadata) is actually destroyed after the organization has commissioned it?	Section
Legislation / Legal		
LL-01	Is the cloud service provider responsible for providing the service?	Yes / No
LL-02	Who is responsible for providing the service?	Section

#	Criteria	Form
LL-03	Under which conditions can agreements be changed?	Section
LL-04	Are pre-changes announced in terms of conditions?	Yes / No
LL-05	What is the minimum period held for changes to terms?	Section
LL-06	Is the customers' approval agreement necessary for changing the terms?	Yes / No
LL-07	What happens if change in terms is not accepted?	Section
LL-08	Under what conditions can customers terminate their agreement in the meantime?	Section
LL-09	Are there "acceptable use policies" for customers that can lead to customer service termination?	Yes / No
LL-10	Is there a recovery period in case of deviation from these "acceptable use policies"?	Yes / No
LL-11	How long is this recovery period?	Section
LL-12	Does the contract fall under Dutch law?	Yes / No
LL-13	What law is applicable to the service of the cloud service provider?	Section
LL-14	Can disputes be settled in the Netherlands?	Yes / No
LL-15	Is Safe Harbour applicable to the contract and / or cloud service provider?	Yes / No
LL-16	Is the Patriot Act applicable to the contract and / or the cloud service provider?	Yes / No
LL-17	Does the contract signature take place before the service is commenced?	Yes / No
LL-18	Is arbitration preferred, over right?	Yes / No
LL-19	What is the liable of the cloud service provider?	Section
Price		
PR-01	Does the cloud service provider use a unit-based pricing model?	Yes / No
PR-02	What periods are used for the pricing model (per hour, month, year et cetera.)?	Section
PR-03	Based on which units are counted (users, transactions or data)?	Section
PR-04	What are your prices per unit / period (e.g. bronze 10 Euro / month - silver 20 Euro / month)?	Section
PR-05	Is there a unit price?	Yes / No
PR-06	How does this quantity discount look like this?	Section
PR-07	Are there any costs on termination of service (exit strategy)?	Yes / No
PR-08	Are there any costs for data retention or data extraction?	Yes / No
PR-09	Are there any costs for transfer / migration?	Yes / No
PR-10	Are the costs elastic (both for more and less)?	Yes / No
PR-11	Are there additional options that can involve additional costs?	Yes / No
PR-12	What are these options?	Section
PR-13	What are the costs for these?	Section
PR-14	What costs are variable without the user's direct impact (e.g. bandwidth or system data storage that automatically expands)?	Section
SLA		
SL-01	Is a customer immediately discontinued from at late payment service?	Yes / No
SL-02	What happens when the customer is not paying his payment in time?	Section
SL-03	Are there payment arrangements for payment of overdue payments?	Yes / No

#	Criteria	Form
SL-04	Is there a service desk for users?	Yes / No
SL-05	Is there a service desk for (functional) support?	Yes / No
SL-06	Is the cloud service provider responsible for application management?	Yes / No
SL-07	Is the cloud service provider responsible for technical management?	Yes / No
SL-08	What opening hours does the cloud service provider use?	Section
SL-09	What response times does the cloud service provider help desk use?	Section
SL-10	What handling times do the cloud service provider help desk use?	Section
SL-11	How is the handling of calamities and malfunctions?	Section
SL-12	How does this handling take place?	Section
SL-13	How are the customers informed in case of calamities and malfunctions?	Yes / No
SL-14	What reports does the cloud service provider provide?	Section
SL-15	What happens if (unexpectedly) the data of the customers, that is under the control of the cloud service provider, are lost?	Section
SL-16	To what extent does the cloud service provider follow the use of the service provided by the institution?	Section
SL-17	Are the reports available?	Yes / No
SL-18	How are these reports available?	Section
SL-19	Which metadata (specific usage data) are defined by the provider, who will be shared and under what conditions?	Section
SL-20	With whom is this data shared and under what conditions?	Section
SL-21	Has a bonus / malus arrangement been defined?	Yes / No
SL-22	How does the bonus / malus arrangement work?	Section
SL-23	What procedures and warranties does the cloud service provider have for backup and recovery?	Section
SL-24	Can this be tested periodically by the organization?	Yes / No
SL-25	What goodness is there for backup and recovery (individual, group and organization)?	Section
SL-26	Can the cloud service provider data resell or transfer (un)anonymous the data to third parties?	Yes / No
SL-27	If so, what are the conditions for this?	Section
SL-28	Are there any free options?	Yes / No
SL-29	Are there trial options?	Yes / No
SL-30	Are there performance criteria?	Yes / No
SL-31	Does the cloud service provider support services use?	Yes / No
SL-32	Is real-time management info available?	Yes / No
SL-33	May and can an external party monitor the cloud service provider?	Yes / No
SL-34	Is the service desk suitable for the broker?	Yes / No
Payment		
PM-01	Does the cloud service provider use a compound billing option?	Text box
PM-02	Is there a minimum contract period?	Section
PM-03	What payment options does the cloud service provider use (credit card, bank, PayPal, invoice)?	Section
PM-04	Is payment by bank possible?	Yes / No

#	Criteria	Form
PM-05	Is there a detailed invoice on unit level available?	Yes / No
Security		
SE-01	What security statements does the cloud service provider have?	Section
SE-02	What is the validity of these statements?	Section
SE-03	Is there a well-documented assessment of the cloud service provider's development process by an independent expert?	Yes / No
SE-04	Can a periodic review of the cloud service provider's processes be performed by an independent expert?	Yes / No
SE-05	How are your employees screened?	Section
SE-06	What is the achieved Capability Maturity Model Integration (CMMI) level?	Section
SE-07	Which ITIL certificates does the cloud service provider have?	Section
SE-08	What qualifications do the cloud service provider employees have (ITIL, Microsoft certificates, CCISP, education level) have?	Section
SE-09	Is there a form of implementation of business continuity management, preferably based on BS 259997 and indicating that crisis situations are being tested regularly?	Section
SE-10	Does the cloud service provider comply with PCI (an American Payment Card Industry Security Directive)?	Yes / No
SE-11	What security procedures does the cloud service provider have internally?	Section
SE-12	How does the cloud service provider deal with urgent notifications such as virus warnings, Distributed Denial-Of-Service (DDOS), suspicious patterns, et cetera.?	Section
SE-13	Which subcontractors are deployed by the cloud service provider that are part of the total service? (So no suppliers not involved in the operational service).	Section
SE-14	What security agreements does the cloud service provider have with its subcontractors?	Section
SE-15	Does the cloud service provider have a formal approved information security policy based on or comparable to the information security code (ISO 27001/27002)?	Yes / No
SE-16	Is there an annual report on the effectiveness of the policy? (Indicate when last reported)	Yes / No
SE-17	Do the cloud service providers' employees have a defined confidentiality obligation?	Yes / No
SE-18	Is the administration of resources (hard & software) complete and correct?	Yes / No
SE-19	Is there a secretive duty and code of conduct communicated with the employees?	Yes / No
SE-20	Has the staff with access to the systems / data on a statement about the behaviour?	Yes / No
SE-21	How is changing users and usage settled?	Section
SE-22	How does the cloud service provider deal with security fixes?	Section
SE-23	Can the customer choose to turn on or off beta functionality?	Yes / No
SE-24	Which chain dependency does the cloud service provider have? What is the way in which the security in the chain is configured?	Section

Table 13-1, Programme of requirements.

13.2 Check list cloud UC

The following abbreviations are used in the header of the table below:

- # = Chapter in the UC template
- R# = Risk as designated in Chapters 7 and 12.
- I = IaaS
- P = PaaS
- S = SaaS

If a risk is to be controlled in an IaaS, PaaS and / or SaaS cloud SLA then this is indicated by a '+', '0' or '-' sign. A '+' sign means that this is very important, a '-' sign indicates that this is not important at all. An '0' indicates that this depends on the situation.

#	Subject	R#	Checkpoint	I	P	S
1. General						
1	General		Is there a brief description of the content and composition of this document?	0	0	0
1.1	Goal		Is the objective of the contract appointed?	0	0	0
1.2.1	Related documents		Is there a reference to the related documents?	0	0	0
1.2.2	Related documents		Is a rank order for the mentioned documents indicated?	0	0	0
2. Structure of the contract						
2	Structure of the contract		Is the structure of the contract described?	0	0	0
2.1	Date of commencement of contract		Has the date of entry been appointed?	0	0	0
2.2	Maintenance of the contract		Is the maintenance of the contract established?	0	0	0
Article 1. Glossary						
Art 1	Glossary		Are the specific terms used in the contract defined?	0	0	0
Article 2. Object of agreement						
Art 2	Object of agreement		What is the domain of the contract, what is the matter and what is not covered?	0	0	0
Article 3. Duration of the agreement						
Art 3	Date and time of entry		Is the start date and the term (end date) of the contract appointed?	0	0	0
Article 4. Cooperation by the parties						
Art 4.1	Engaged third parties	R1.5	Are his requirements regarding the commitment of third parties established?	+	+	+
Art 4.2	Engaged suppliers	R1.5	Have there been agreements about the commitment of suppliers?	+	+	+
Art 4.3	Liability and ownership	R1.12	Is it guaranteed that third party efforts are made known to ensure confusion of liability and ownership (holes or overlaps)?	+	+	+
Art 4.4	Access data	R1.2	Is it arranged that the customer gives third parties permission to have access to the data?	+	+	+

#	Subject	R#	Checkpoint	I	P	S
Art 4.5	Exclusion Access		Is it arranged that there is access in case of exclusion?	+	+	+
Article 5. Delivery						
Art 5	Terms of delivery		Are the delivery terms defined / included?	0	0	0
Article 6. Acceptance						
Art 6.1	Acceptance procedure		Has the acceptance procedure been established?	-	+	+
Art 6.2	Acceptance tests	R3.9	Are acceptance tests performed?	-	+	+
Art 6.3	Repair application	R5.2	Are there any acceptance tests for the recovery of an application?	-	-	+
Article 7. Warranty						
Art 7	Warranty		Is the warranty procedure determined?	-	+	+
Article 8. Liability						
Art 8.1	Determination of liability		Is the cloud service provider's liability established?	+	+	+
Art 8.2	Compensation	R3.9	Has a compensation been agreed in case of damage?	+	+	+
Art 8.3	Licenses		Is the liability for licenses recorded?	+	+	+
Article 9. Prices, bonus / malus						
Art 9.1	Prices		Have the prizes been defined?	0	0	0
Art 9.2	Fines		Is determined how to deal with fines?	0	0	0
Article 10. Payments						
Art 10.1	VAT and price guarantees		Are VAT and price guarantee set?	0	0	0
Art 10.2	Payment Rules		Is the payment subject to rules such as: payment period, billing information, settlement, exceedance, et cetera?	0	0	0
Article 11a. Intellectual property rights						
Art 11.1	Intellectual property rights		Is it determined who has intellectual property rights?	-	-	+
Article 11b. Data ownership						
Art 11.2	Claim ownership	R3.5	Has the data ownership been claimed and captured?	+	+	+
Art 11.3	Data usage	R3.5	Has data usage been captured?	-	-	+
Art 11.4	Data types	R3.5	Has a distinction been made between data types such as business data, metadata and management data?	-	-	+
Art 11.5	Location	R3.6	Is contractually agreed where the location of the data, backup data and management data is?	+	-	-
Art 11.6	Data integrity	R3.9	Is the cloud service provider audited on the effectiveness and efficiency of data integrity management measures such as: ETL exceptions, ACID, Error handling, managing dead letter boxes?	-	-	+
Art 11.7	Destruction hardware		Have there been any agreements about the destruction of hardware?	+	-	-

#	Subject	R#	Checkpoint	I	P	S
Art 11.8	Exclusivity		Are there any agreements regarding exclusivity?	+	+	+
Article 12. Confidentiality and Security						
Art 12	Confidentiality		Are there any conditions defined regarding secrecy and security?	0	0	0
Article 13. Assurance						
Art 13	Liability		Are there any conditions defined regarding insurance such as civil liability, premium and liability?	0	0	0
Article 14. Transfer rights and duties						
Art 14	Transfer rights and duties		Have there been agreements regarding the transfer of rights and obligations?	0	0	0
Article 15. Force majeure						
Art 15	Force majeure		Is it determined when there is force majeure and what should be settled?	0	0	0
Article 16. Decomposition						
Art 16.1	Decomposition conditions		Is it determined when / under which conditions the contract is terminated?	0	0	0
Art 16.2	Exit Strategy	R1.9	Has an exit strategy been drawn up?	+	+	+
Art 16.3	Exit Strategy Plan	R1.9	Has an exit strategy plan been drawn up?	+	+	+
Art 16.4	Escrow arrangement	R1.9	Has an escrow arrangement been drawn up?	-	+	+
Art 16.5	Transfer information	R1.9	Is it stipulated that customer data must be transferred in the format provided by the customer?	-	-	+
Art 16.6	Destruction certificate	R1.9	Has the cloud service provider been destroying data and issuing a destruction certificate?	+	+	+
Art 16.7	Documentation	R1.9	Has it been established that the cloud service provider documents the service so that it is adopted by a third party within 3 months?	-	+	+
Art 16.8	Continuation service free of charge	R1.9	Is it established that the cloud service provider makes sure that the service is granted free of charge if the third party cannot continue the service within the stated 3 months due to demonstrable defects in the documentation?	-	+	+
Art 16.9	Capture of rights	R3.4	Are the rights to retrieve this data recorded: what data, how fast, in what form?	+	+	+
Article 17 Disputes, applicable law and forum choice						
Art 17	Disputes		Is it clear how disputes are dealt with?	0	0	0
Article 18 The service provisioning						
Art 18	Description		Are the services / products described?	0	0	0
Article 19 General						
Art 19.1	General		Is the merger clause applicable?	0	0	0

#	Subject	R#	Checkpoint	I	P	S
Art 19.2	General		Are the applicable legal frameworks indicated?	0	0	0
Article 20 Others						
Art 20	Others	R1.6	Has the contract been reviewed by a lawyer?	+	+	+
Art 20	Others		Has a TPM been agreed on?	+	+	+

Table 13-2, Check list Cloud UC.

13.3 Check list Cloud SLA

#	Subject	R#	Checkpoint	I	P	S
1. General						
1	General		Is there a brief description of the content and composition of this document?	0	0	0
1.1	Subject of the agreement		Is the subject of the agreement formulated?	0	0	0
1.2.1	Parties, Declaration and Signature		Are the parties appointed?	0	0	0
1.2.2	Parties, Declaration and Signature		Is the SLA signed?	0	0	0
1.3	Purpose of the SLA		Has the SLA's objective been formulated?	0	0	0
1.4.1	Commencement and maturity		Is the SLA's start date and term (end date) formulated?	0	0	0
1.4.2	Commencement and maturity		Has been described on the basis of which the SLA can be dissolved?	0	0	0
1.5	Terms		Are the specific terms used in the SLA defined?	0	0	0
1.6	Related documents		Is there a reference to the related documents?	0	0	0
1.7	Service Description		Are the services described?	0	0	0
1.8	Result obligation		Is there a statement of effort / result obligation?	0	0	0
1.9	Control and rules		Is it described how control and rules have been regulated?	0	0	0
1.10	Service opening hours and service maintenance hours		Are the opening hours and service maintenance times formulated?	-	-	+
1.11	Work agreements and procedures		Have there been any employment agreements and procedures?	-	-	+
1.12	Document management		Has been described how the SLA will be maintained, who / what / when?	0	0	0
2. Description of service						
2	Description of service		Has been described what the domain of the SLA is, what is covered and what is not covered?	0	0	0
2	Description of service		Is it described at which locations the service is taking place?	-	-	-

#	Subject	R#	Checkpoint	I	P	S
2	Description of service		Are the services / products included in the service catalogue?	0	0	0
2.1	Introduction		Has it been briefly stated what the description of the service should contribute?	0	0	0
2.2	General description of the service		Is there a general description of the service?	0	0	0
2.3.1	Service Description		Are the services / products described?	0	0	0
2.3.2	Service Description	R1.5	Is information processing chain defined and checked?	0	0	0
3. Performance Agreements						
3	Performance Agreements		Are the performance indicators and performance norms measurable?	0	0	0
3	Performance Agreements		Is it recorded how performance is measured?	0	0	0
3.1	Introduction		Is there an explanation of the intention of the performance agreements?	0	0	0
3.2.1	Product Performance Indicators		Have there been agreements at the product level?	0	0	0
3.2.2	Product Performance Indicators		Are there any agreements about the maximum scalability and timeliness on the scale of the solution?	+	+	+
3.2.3	Product Performance Indicators		Are there any agreements about the frequency of firmware upgrades?	+	-	-
3.3.1	Process performance indicators		Are there agreements at process level?	0	+	+
3.3.2	Process performance indicators		Have there been agreements about lifecycle management (release management and version control)?	-	+	+
3.3.3	Process performance indicators		Are there any agreements about the D-T-A times?	-	+	+
3.4.1	Service Performance Indicators		Are there any conditions for the RPO and RTO?	+	+	+
3.4.2	Service performance indicators	R3.11	Are there any agreements about the frequency of the DRP?	+	+	+
3.4.3	Service Performance Indicators	R4.2	Are there any agreements about volume adjustment, such as maximum data streams, fluctuation, request for more capacity, et cetera.?	-	-	+
3.4.4	Service Performance Indicators	R4.2	Are there any agreements regarding the one-time processing of data regarding request time and frequency?	-	-	+
3.4.5	Service Performance Indicators	R4.2	Are there any agreements about the frequency and volume of data exports?	-	-	+
3.4.6	Service Performance Indicators	R4.2	Are there any agreements about the rate at which data streams can be changed?	-	-	+
3.4.7	Service Performance Indicators	R6.2	Has a frequency of a PEN test been agreed?	+	+	+
3.4.8	Service Performance Indicators	R6.7	Have recovery times been formulated in case of a vulnerability?	+	+	+

#	Subject	R#	Checkpoint	I	P	S
3.4.9	Service Performance Indicators	R6.9	Is the CIA rating per service classified?	+	+	+
3.4.10	Service Performance Indicators	R7.8	Have there been norms on the D-T-A environments?	+	-	+
3.4.11	Service Performance Indicators		Have there been any agreements about the service continuity?	+	+	+
3.4.12	Service Performance Indicators		Are there any agreements regarding availability?	+	+	+
3.5	Administrative performance indicators		Have there been agreements regarding the delivery of information that can be used by the customer to manage at a higher level, such as balanced scorecard information?	-	-	+
3.6.1	Confidentiality Performance Indicators		Are there any agreements regarding the delivery of use by whitelisted users?	-	+	+
3.6.2	Confidentiality Performance Indicators		Are there any agreements about access to the keys that store encrypted company data?	-	+	+
3.6.3	Integrity performance indicators		Are there any agreements regarding the delivery of mutation data by whitelisted users?	-	+	+
3.6.4	Integrity performance indicators		Are there any agreements regarding the delivery of the logged privileged users' activities?	-	+	+
3.6.5	Integrity performance indicators		Have there been agreements about the delivery of regular behavioural patterns and tolerated abnormalities?	-	+	+
3.6.6	Availability Performance Indicators		Are there any agreements regarding the delivery of data on outbound detected attempts at disturbance?	-	+	+
3.6.7	Availability Performance Indicators		Are there any agreements regarding the provision of data about denying access to whitelisted (Privileged) Users based on endpoint security requirements?	-	+	+
3.6.8	CERT performance indicators		Are there any agreements about the tasks, responsibilities and powers of the cloud service provider towards the CERT organization?	-	+	+
4. Service report						
4	Service Reporting		Has a service reporting frequency been formulated?	+	+	+
4.1	Introduction		Is there an explanation of the intention of the service report?	0	0	0
4.2	Lead reporting		Are there direct control data formulated like escalation times?	0	0	0
4.2.1	Lead reporting		Are there any agreements regarding the timeliness of event notifications?	+	+	-
4.3	Team reporting		Are there control data that are periodically viewed as capacity utilization?	+	+	+

#	Subject	R#	Checkpoint	I	P	S
5. Communication						
5	Communication		Is the meeting structure determined?	-	-	-
5	Communication		Is the frequency of the report determined?	-	-	-
5.1	Introduction		-	-	-	-
5.2.1	Operational meeting		Has a point of contact for both parties been defined?	-	-	-
5.2.2	Operational meeting	R7.3	Are the agreements about the scheduled maintenance on the agenda?	-	-	-
5.2.3	Operational meeting		Are there any agreements regarding a direct feedback / reporting in case of security incidents and the handling of a priority 1 handling of this type of incident?	+	+	+
5.3	Escalation meeting		Has an escalation meeting agreement been reached?	0	0	0
5.4	Tactical meeting		Has a tactical meeting been agreed?	-	0	+
5.5.1	Strategic meeting		Has a strategic meeting been reached?	-	0	+
5.5.2	Strategic meeting	R7.1	Is there a meeting about the choices of products and services in the long term?	+	+	+
5.5.3	Strategic meeting	R7.2	Is there a N-1 policy for life cycle management?	+	+	+
5.6	Service meeting		Is it recorded how / what information the customer provides to the cloud service provider?	-	-	-
5.7	Evaluation SLA		Is there an evaluation frequency included in the SLA?	-	-	-
5.8	Participants in the service meeting		Is it known who the participants are in the service meeting (officials)?	-	-	-
5.9	Contacts, Responsibilities and Addresses		Are there any contacts, responsibilities and addresses appointed or included in the DAP?	-	-	-
6. Mutual obligations						
6	Mutual obligations		-			
6.1	Introduction		Is there an explanation of the intention of mutual obligations?	0	0	0
6.2	Execution		Is the service described in general?	0	0	0
6.3	Information		Are his agreements regarding maintenance and the like described?	0	0	0
6.4	Occupancy staff		Are there any agreements about the staff's occupancy?	-	-	-
6.5	Good homage		Are there any demands made on the customer like good home affairs?	0	0	0
6.6	Legal frameworks		Are the applicable legal frameworks indicated?	+	+	+
7. Terms and Conditions						
7	Terms and Conditions		Is determined how to deal with fines?	0	0	0

#	Subject	R#	Checkpoint	I	P	S
7.1	Limitations, Dependencies and Force Majeure		Is it formulated when there is a force majeure and what should be settled?	0	0	0
7.2	Disputes		Has a disputes committee been appointed?	0	0	0
7.3	Rules and Standards		Are the rules and standards to be applied?	+	+	+
7.4	Copyright		Is the copyright granted?	-	-	-
7.5	Software License		Are there any agreements about the software licenses?	+	+	+
7.6	Confidentiality		Is the confidentiality regulated?	+	+	+
7.7.1	Accountability and control		Has the frequency of accountability been agreed?	+	+	+
7.7.2	Accountability and control		Have there been agreements about the audit of accountability?	+	+	+
7.7.3	Accountability and control		Is it determined how to handle availability of third parties?	0	0	0
7.7.4	Accountability and control	R1.1	Is a TPM delivery required?	+	+	+
7.7.5	Accountability and control	R1.1	Is an ISAE 3402 required?	+	+	+
7.7.6	Accountability and control	R1.1	Has a US-EU Safe Harbour statement been drawn up?	+	+	+
7.7.7	Accountability and control	R1.10	Does the cloud service provider comply with the Personal Data Protection Act (WBP)?	+	+	+
7.7.8	Accountability and control	R1.11	Is there a right of audit included?	+	+	+
7.7.9	Accountability and control	R6.6	Has a PCI DSS audit been agreed?	+	+	+
	Appendix 1: Change sheet		Is an attachment included to keep track of changes to the SLA?	0	0	0
	Appendix 2: Underlying contracts		Is there reference to underlying contracts?	0	0	0

Table 13-3, Check list Cloud SLA.

13.4 Check list Cloud DFA

#	Subject	R#	Checkpoint	I	P	S
1. General						
1	General		Is there a brief description of the content and composition of this document?	0	0	0
1.1	Purpose		Is the purpose described in the DFA?	0	0	0
1.2	Target audience		Is the target group of the document appointed?	0	0	0
1.3	Reading guideline		Has a reading guideline been included in the DFA?	0	0	0
1.4	Basis		Is it described why the DFA has been formulated?	0	0	0

#	Subject	R#	Checkpoint	I	P	S
1.5	Related documents		Are the related documents described?	0	0	0
2. Agreements						
2	Agreements		Have there been general agreements on the financial settlement?	0	0	0
2.1	Price Policy		Is the price policy formulated?	0	0	0
2.2	Price per service		Is the price structure transparent to the customer?	0	0	0
2.3.1	Price calculation		Is the price calculation transparent to the customer?	0	0	0
2.3.2	Price calculation	R2.2 R2.4	Have the scenarios been calculated in advance (costs, growth, shrinkage et cetera.)?	+	+	+
2.3.3	Price calculation	R2.2	In the event of a tendering procedure, in any case, is a three-year accounting period adopted?	+	+	+
2.3.4	Price calculation	R2.3	Are all direct and indirect costs of cloud services determined, especially the adaptive costs may be higher?	+	+	+
2.3.5	Price calculation	R2.3	Are the costs based on the process / procedure / task demarcation?	+	+	+
2.4.1	Bonus / Malus		Is there a bonus / malus arrangement?	0	0	0
2.4.2	Bonus / Malus		Is it indicated under what conditions the bonus / malus is awarded?	0	0	0
2.4.3	Bonus / Malus		Is there a maximum associated with the bonus / malus?	0	0	0
2.5.1	Billing		Have all billing information been agreed on?	0	0	0
2.5.2	Billing	R1.7	Are there any agreements regarding payment terms and signalling to prevent termination?	+	+	+
2.5.3	Billing	R1.7	Is there a control defined on the strict monitoring of payments?	+	+	+
2.5.4	Billing	R2.1	Has it been determined beforehand how the cloud service can be settled internally (at the customer)?	+	+	+
2.5.5	Billing	R2.1	Has the cloud service provider, if possible, been tuned in advance how these can be settled internally?	+	+	+

Table 13-4, Check list Cloud DFA.

13.5 Check list Cloud DAP

#	Subject	R#	Checkpoint	I	P	S
1. General						
1	General		Is there a brief description of the content and composition of this document?	0	0	0
1.1	Purpose		Is the purpose of the DAP formulated?	0	0	0
1.2	Target audience		Is the target group of the document defined?	0	0	0

#	Subject	R#	Checkpoint	I	P	S
1.3	Reading guideline		Is the reading guideline included in the DAP?	0	0	0
1.4	Basis		Is it described why the DAP has been handled?	0	0	0
1.5	Related documents		Are the related documents described?	0	0	0
2. Document management						
2	Document management		Is document management configured in DAP?	0	0	0
2.1	General		Is the meaning of this chapter described?	0	0	0
2.2.1	DAP Change Procedure		Is the DAP change procedure included?	0	0	0
2.2.2	DAP Change Procedure		Has a DAP change form been included?	0	0	0
2.2.1	Concept		Is there a DAP concept?	0	0	0
2.2.2	Changes		Is the control of all relevant documents described?	0	0	0
2.2.3	DAP Procedure Changes		Is there a change procedure in the DAP?	0	0	0
2.2.4	Extension and Termination DAP		Is it described how DAP extension and termination takes place?	0	0	0
2.2.5	Incidental DAP Disorders		Has been indicated how to handle incidental divergences on the DAP?	0	0	0
2.3	Quality assurance		Is it described how quality control of the DAP is organized?	0	0	0
3. Communication						
3	Communication		Is it described how the communication lines run?	0	0	0
3.1.1	Contact person		Are the contacts described?	0	0	0
3.1.2	Contact person		Are the addresses of the parties involved included?	0	0	0
3.2	Escalation and calamities		Are the escalation lines described?	0	0	0
3.3.1	Complaints discussion		Are the dispute rules described?	0	0	0
3.3.2	Complaints discussion		Has the complaint process been described?	0	0	0
3.4	Contract documents		Has established and established the contract, the SLA and the DAP?	0	0	0
3.5	Meeting structures, composition and frequency		Have the meetings been described?	0	0	0
4. Work area						
4	Scope		Has it been established what the scope of the DAP is?	0	0	0
4.1	Management processes		Has a procedural demarcation been identified per process?	0	0	0
4.2.1	Management tasks		Are the tasks, responsibilities and authorizations of qualifications described?	0	0	0

#	Subject	R#	Checkpoint	I	P	S
4.2.2	Management tasks	R3.8	Have management tasks been agreed on related to the reference integrity?	-	-	+
4.2.3	Management tasks	R3.8	Have management tasks been agreed on maintaining the business rules?	-	-	+
4.2.4	Management tasks	R3.8	Have management tasks been agreed on the quality of data and control parameters such as accuracy, completeness, timeliness and up-to-date?	-	-	+
4.2.5	Management tasks	R3.11	Have there been any agreements regarding recovery tests?	+	+	+
4.2.6	Management tasks	R3.11	Are there any agreements about what is included in a DRP and how to implement it?	+	+	+
4.2.7	Management tasks	R4.1	Have there been agreements about the extensibility of functionality such as business rules?	-	-	+
4.2.8	Management tasks	R4.2	Are there any agreements about adjusting volumes?	+	+	+
4.2.9	Management tasks	R4.2	Have there been any agreements regarding the monitoring of ETL errors?	-	-	+
4.2.10	Management tasks	R4.3	Are there any agreements regarding how data is delivered?	-	-	+
4.2.11	Management tasks	R4.3	Are there any agreements about one-time processing, how to execute and what information should be transferred for execution?	-	-	+
4.2.12	Management tasks	R4.3	Are there any agreements regarding how data exports can be requested and what the data formats are there?	-	-	+
4.2.13	Management tasks	R4.3	Have there been agreements regarding the controllability of data streams such as how and where to set them or how to apply for it?	-	-	+
4.2.14	Management tasks	R5.2	Is determined how an application has to be restored?	-	+	+
4.2.15	Management tasks	R5.2	Is there a complete test after recovery of the application?	-	+	+
4.2.16	Management tasks	R5.2	Is the recoverability of the application included in the DRP?	-	+	+
4.2.17	Management tasks	R6.2	Has the network been included in the DRP?	+	-	-
4.2.18	Management tasks	R6.4	Has it been agreed how local support is available for emergency situations?	+	+	+
4.2.19	Management tasks	R6.6	Has the platform test been included in the PEN test?	-	+	-
4.2.20	Management tasks	R6.7	Is the virtualization on leakage tested in the PEN test or by an expert review?	+	-	-
4.2.21	Management tasks	R6.8	Is QoS adjustable and flexible?	+	-	-
4.2.22	Management tasks	R6.11	Has the PaaS vulnerability been included in the PEN test?	-	+	-

#	Subject	R#	Checkpoint	I	P	S
4.2.23	Management tasks	R7.5	Are there any agreements on the DTAP procedures like the promotion of A to P?	-	+	+
4.2.24	Management tasks	R7.6	Are there any agreements about the facilities of the A environment like rights, data encryption and data scrambling?	-	+	+
4.2.25	Management tasks	R7.7	Have there been any agreements regarding the handling of security incidents?	+	+	+
4.3.1	Responsibility	R4.2	Are the roles of the parties involved described?	+	+	+
4.3.2	Responsibility		Are the natural persons described by role?	0	0	0
4.4	Powers		Has been described who the owner, manager and performer is per process?	0	0	0
5. Agreements support process						
5	Agreement support process (one chapter per management process)		-			
5.1	The interfaces	R1.4	Has the governance organization and control been explicitly approved?	+	+	+
5.2	Explanation		Has an explanation been given about the procedure interaction?	0	0	0
5.3	Appointments		Are there any agreements regarding the processes (per procedure)?	0	0	0
5.4.1	Reports		Are the templates of the agreed reports included?	0	0	0
5.4.2	Reports	R6.5	Are there any agreements regarding event / incident reporting in case of a disturbance that needs to be solved at the customer and what information is required from the cloud service provider?	+	+	+
5.4.3	Reports	R6.5	Is the monitor information about access to the computer centre claimable?	+	+	+
Appendices						
Attach-ment 1	Change sheet		Has an overview of recognized standard changes been included?	0	0	0
Appen-dix 2	Planned maintenance	R7.4	Is the planned maintenance described?	+	+	+
Attach-ment 3	Functions & Persons		Are the functions and persons defined?	0	0	0

Table 13-5, Check list Cloud DAP.

13.6 Check list Cloud ESS

#	Subject	R#	Checkpoint	I	P	S
1. General						
1	General		Is there a brief description of the content and composition of this document?	0	0	0

#	Subject	R#	Checkpoint	I	P	S
1.1.1	External spec sheet requirements	R1.8	Has a Plan of Requirements been drawn up?	+	+	+
1.1.2	External spec sheet requirements	R4.3	Is segregation of duties in the PoR included?	+	+	+
1.1.3	External spec sheet requirements	R4.3	Has fraud been included in the ESS?	-	-	+
1.1.4	External spec sheet requirements	R4.3	Are the SSO requirements determined in the ESS, such as broker service, identity management platforms in the form of a PaaS and federative directory solutions using the content of the on-premise directory structure is used in the cloud?	-	+	-
1.1.5	External spec sheet requirements	R6.8	Is the ESS included in the list of required management protocols?	+	+	-
1.1.6	External spec sheet requirements	R6.8	Are there any requirements for the scalability of the bandwidth?	+	-	-
1.1.7	External spec sheet requirements	R6.8	Are there any requirements for the exclusivity of the network or QoS?	+	-	-
1.1.8	External spec sheet requirements	R6.8	Are there any requirements for QoS flexibility?	+	-	-
1.1.9	External spec sheet requirements	R6.8	Are there any requirements on the security of the logical network?	+	-	-
1.1.10	External spec sheet requirements	R6.9	Is the CIA rating included in the security plan with countermeasures?	+	+	+
1.1.11	External spec sheet requirements	R6.10	Is directory services for identity management formulated?	-	+	-
1.1.12	External spec sheet requirements	R6.11	Is a penetration test for the PaaS solution demanded?	-	+	-

Table 13-6, Check list Cloud ESS.

13.7 Check list Cloud ISS

#	Subject	R#	Checkpoint	I	P	S
1. General						
1	General		Is there a brief description of the content and composition of this document?	0	0	0
1.1.1	Internal spec sheet requirements	R3.8	Has the cloud service provider drawn up a security plan to realize the measures of the CIA requirements?	+	+	+
1.1.2	Internal spec sheet requirements	R3.9	Have there been repressive measures formulated in the event of failure of the information security?	+	+	+
1.1.3	Internal spec sheet requirements	R3.10	Are there exclusivity requirements about the data layer like an own database?	+	-	-
1.1.4	Internal spec sheet requirements	R4.4	Is it clear how authenticity and authorization are regulated, especially the interaction with those of the customer?	-	+	-
1.1.5	Internal spec sheet requirements	R5.1	Are there exclusivity requirements about the application layer formulated like its own runtime environment?	-	+	-

#	Subject	R#	Checkpoint	I	P	S
1.1.6	Internal spec sheet requirements	R5.2	Are there requirements formulated how the environment is being restored, e.g. A virtual platform recovery)?	-	+	-
1.1.7	Internal spec sheet requirements	R6.1	Are there exclusivity requirements formulated about the network layer such as its own connection or Virtual Local Area Network (VLAN)?	+	-	-
1.1.8	Internal spec sheet requirements	R6.3	Has it been described which measures need to be taken against hacking, such as a PEN test by a reputable company and have the countermeasures been effected?	+	+	+
1.1.9	Internal spec sheet requirements	R6.4	Are there exclusions to the stated requirements and are countermeasures for all risks formulated?	+	+	+
1.1.10	Internal spec sheet requirements	R6.6	Are the limitations of platform services defined?	-	+	-
1.1.11	Internal spec sheet requirements	R6.8	Is there a security measure for the logical network?	+	-	-

Table 13-7, Check list Cloud ISS.

Appendices

Appendix A, Literature list

Reference	Publication
Best 2011	B. de Best, "ICT prestatie indicator", Dutch language, Leonon Media 2011, ISBN13: 978 90 71501 470.
Best 2012	B. de Best, "Quality Control & Assurance", Dutch language, Leonon Media 2012, ISBN13: 978 90 71501 531.
Best 2013	B. de Best, "SLA Best Practices", Dutch language, Leonon Media 2013, ISBN-13: 978 90 71501 456, second edition.
Best 2014a	B. de Best, "Acceptatiecriteria", Dutch language, Leonon Media, ISBN 13: 978 90 71501 784, 2014, second edition.
Best 2014b	B. de Best, "Agile Service Management met Scrum", Dutch language, Leonon Media, ISBN13: 978 90 71501 807, 2014.
Best 2015a	B. de Best, "Agile Service Management met Scrum in de Praktijk", Dutch language, Leonon Media, ISBN13: 978 90 71501 845, 2015.
Best 2015b	B. de Best, "Ketenbeheer in de praktijk", Dutch language, Leonon Media, ISBN13: 978 90 71501 852, 2015, second edition.
Best 2017a	B. de Best, "Beheren onder Architectuur", Dutch language, Leonon Media 2017, ISBN13: 978 90 71501 913, second edition.
Best 2017b	B. de Best, "SLA Templates", Leonon Media, English language, ISBN13: 978 94 92618 030, 2017.
Best 2017c	B. de Best, "DevOps Best Practices", Leonon Media, English language, ISBN13: 978 94 92618 078, 2017.
Coul 2001	J.C. Op de Coul, "Taken, Functies, Rollen en Competenties in de Informatica", ten Hagen & Stam Uitgevers, 2001, ISBN 90 44003 437.
ITINFRA 2010-3	B. de Best, Article in IT Infra 2010 nr 3. "Zo worden service normen meetbaar".
ITINFRA 2010-4	B. de Best, Article in IT Infra 2010 nr 4. "Zo geef je monitor-architectuur vorm".
Looijen 2014	M. Looijen, L. van Hemmen, "Beheer van Informatiesystemen", zevende druk, Academic Service, 2014, ISBN13: 978 94 62450 936.
Nimwegen 1992	prof. Drs. H. van Nimwegen R.A., "Praktijkgids De Controller & Informatiemanagement afl. 2 (augustus 1992)".
Nimwegen 1993	prof. Drs. H. van Nimwegen R.A., "Administratieve processen vastleggen, verbeteren en ontwikkelen", Kluwer Bedrijfswetenschappen, Deventer, 1993, ISBN 90 267 1688 5.
Cabinet Office 2011 SS	Cabinet Office, "Service Strategy", ISBN13: 978 01 13313 044.
Cabinet Office 2011 SD	Cabinet Office, "Service Design", ISBN13: 978 01 13313 051.
Cabinet Office 2011 ST	Cabinet Office, "Service Transition", ISBN13: 978 01 13313 068.
Cabinet Office 2011 SO	Cabinet Office, "Service Operation", ISBN13: 978 01 13313 075.
Cabinet Office 2011 CSI	Cabinet Office, "Continual Service Improvement", ISBN13: 978 01 13313 082.
Pascoe 1993	E.I. Pascoe-Samson "Organisatie, Besturing en Informatie", Kluwer Bedrijfswetenschappen, Deventer, 1993.
Pols 2009	R. Van der Pols, "ASL 2 een framework voor applicatiemanagement", tenHagenStam, 2009, ISBN 978 90 87533 120.

Reference	Publication
Pols 2009	R. Van de Pols, "ASL een framework voor applicatiemanagement", Van Haren Publishing, 2009, ISBN13: 978 90 87533 120.
Pols 2011	R. Van der Pols, "BiSL Een framework voor business informatiemanagement", Van Haren Publishing, 2011, ISBN13: 978 90 87536 879.
SABSA 2005	J. Sherwood, A. Clark and D. Lynas, "Enterprise Security Architecture – A Business-Driven Approach", CPM Books, 2005, ISBN13: 978 1 57820 318 5.
Thiadens 1999	T. Thiadens, "Beheer van ICT-voorzieningen", Academic Services, derde herziene uitgave, ISBN 90 39513 902.

Appendix B, Glossary

Underlined words are references to defined terms.

Term	Explanation
Acceptance criteria	This book makes a distinction between generic and specific acceptance criteria, as defined below. **Generic acceptance criteria:** Generic acceptance criteria are the service management requirements that need to be tested. They are defined by the <u>service organization</u> for the use of the ICT products, ICT services, and the products resulting from the service management process implementation such as process designs, procedures and resources, to the extent to which the identified risks are managed. The generic acceptance criteria are based on the CSFs' of the <u>service management processes</u>. These acceptance criteria are called 'generic acceptance criteria' because they are independently defined as much as possible from the information systems. They can (to a certain extent) even be defined independently by choosing a commonly used reference model like ITIL [Best 2014a]. **Specific acceptance criteria:** Specific acceptance criteria are the requirements that need to be tested. They are defined by the <u>user organization</u> for the use of the ICT products and ICT services in order to determine the extent to which the identified risks are controlled. The specific acceptance criteria are based on the CSFs of <u>business processes</u>. These acceptance criteria are called 'Specific Acceptance Criteria', because they must be determined by per organization and even per product [Best 2014a].
American Patriot act	The Patriot Act is an American law aimed at combating terrorism. Under this legislation, the US government and government agencies have far-reaching powers, including forensic research. This implies, among others, that US organizations and companies are obliged to provide access to their infrastructure, such as servers and networks. Business units outside the U.S. territory should also cooperate in the research. That implies concrete that US cloud providers cannot guarantee that data in, for example, Europe cannot be checked by US government services. [Wiki] [ZDNET]. For this reason, it could be forbidden for European authorities to choose an American cloud service provider [Wiki] [Trouw 2011].
Application management	Application management is responsible for maintaining application software and databases [Looijen 2014].
Architecture	The fundamental organization of a system embodied in its compo-nents, their relationships to each other, and to the environment, and the principles guiding its design and evolution [IEEE 2007]. Architecture is a consistent set of principles and models that guide design and realization of the processes, organizational structure, information and technical infrastructure of an organization [Wagter 2002].

Term	Explanation
	To get an information policy into an information plan, a structuring layer is required, so says Boterenbrood. The result of this translation is called architecture [Boterenbrood 2005].
Architecture framework	An architecture framework is a tool for the architect to monitor the coherence between the independent initiatives of an organization. The framework provides the architect with the ability to limit himself to specific elements while designing architecture, while still retaining the overall picture. Within the framework, multiple objects of architecture are distinguished (the sub architectures in the columns) and multiple abstraction levels (the levels in the rows) [Wagter 2002].
Architecture model	Visualization and descriptions of existing and desired situations. Models are the third and lowest level of the architecture framework [Wagter 2002].
Architecture principle	An architecture principle is a guideline or point of departure for a developer, builder or administrator to be taken into consideration during his activities.
Architecture standard	An architecture standard gives a meta level description which an architectural design needs to comply by indicating which components should be recognized, what must be described of a component and what their interrelationship is.
Balanced scorecard	The balanced scorecard is a control model depicting CSFs and Key Performance Indicators (KPIs) in four perspectives, namely: the financial perspective, internal perspective, innovation perspective and customer perspective. This management model is used by many companies in the Netherlands to monitor the chosen strategy.
Business alignment	Align the ICT strategy to the business strategy.
Business domain	A domain in which business processes are based using the information system managed by the service management domain.
Business Process as a Service (BPaaS)	BPaaS is a horizontal or vertical business process that is provided based on the cloud services model. That is considering processes as functions that provide mutual services. For example, performing a credit check as cloud service.
Cloud computing	"The cloud is a network of computer systems that can be utilized by other computers connected to it over the internet. The end user does not know which computer (s) is running the software or where it's exactly located. In this way, the user does not need to be the owner of the hardware and software used and is not responsible for the maintenance. The details of the information technology infrastructure are eliminated and the user has a "own", in size -scalable virtual infrastructure. The cloud is thus a concept that indicates online services. [Wiki].
	Cloud computing is a model for enabling ubiquitous, convenient, on-demand network access to a shared pool of configurable computing resources (e.g., networks, servers, storage, applications, and services) that can be rapidly provisioned and released with minimal management effort or service provider interaction [NIST].
Cloud management	Cloud management concerns the software and technologies designed to manage and monitor applications, data and services in the cloud.

Term	Explanation
	Cloud management tools help a company to ensure that IT resources placed in the cloud work optimally and interact with users and other services.
Cloud marketplace	A cloud marketplace is a place where providers, customers and partners meet. Cloud services are offered here and customers can compare these services to various aspects such as financial, contract, service levels, legal, support and technology. Experience from other users is shared and customers have the opportunity to select from a wide range of services which is the best solution for them.
Cloud Service Broker (CSB)	A viable CSB provider can make it less expensive, easier, safer and more productive for companies to navigate, integrate, consume and extend cloud services, particularly when they span multiple, diverse cloud services providers [Forbes 2012].
Cloud service broker platform	A cloud service broker platform provides extremely integration of cloud services so that they can be offered to customers as a total package. Examples are, the possibility of composite invoices, payment in one currency, support of a first-aid helpdesk, one-time logon of services (SSO) and having a single contact for multiple services.

Cloud service model	The following models of cloud services are recognized: • private cloud service model; • public cloud service model; • hybrid cloud service model; • broker cloud service model.	
	Private cloud service model	In the case of a private cloud service, the services are provided based on an environment exclusively designed for the customer who uses the private service.
	Public cloud Service model	In the event of a public cloud service, the cloud service provider provides the services to various customers using the same facilities.
	Hybrid cloud service model	In the event of a hybrid cloud service, customer service takes place on the basis of a combination of services that are provided by the customer support organization and those that are purchased in the cloud.
	Broker cloud service model	In the case of broker cloud services, the cloud service is provided via an intermediary.

Term	Explanation
Cloud service patterns	A service provided by a cloud service provider. The following distinction for four patterns can be made: • Infrastructure as a Service (IaaS); • Platform as a Service (PaaS); • Software as a Service (SaaS); • Business Process as a Service (BPaaS).
Competence	A competence is a professional skill or personal skill required to perform a task at an appropriate level and / or an employee possesses. Competences are determined by the tasks to be performed in the relevant role and context, respectively, determined by the characteristics of a person in his environment (eg training, training and experience) [Coul 2001]. A competence includes knowledge, skills and attitude.

Term	Explanation
Chain management	Chain management is the collection of service management processes and products that ensure that a set of related and connected business processes function as a whole efficiently and effectively by monitoring (measures) and, where necessary, improving (management). Chain management therefore includes both chain monitoring and chain control.
Chain control	Chain control includes the defining of chains, making agreements about the functionality and quality of the chain and the (automatic) intervention at the time the chain agreements are not met [Best 2015b].
Component Failure Impact Analysis (CFIA)	CFIA is an analysis technique that links a ICT service to the ICT involved components. On the basis of this analysis, weaknesses in the ICT infrastructure can be found and countermeasures can be taken.
Chain monitoring	Chain monitoring is the measurement of a chain. The chain can be defined on three levels. • a chain of infrastructural resources (networks plus transport protocols); • a chain of information systems (applications plus application communication); • a chain of information (data flows through business processes) [Best 2015b].
Critical Success Factor	A CSF describes a possible cause of failure to achieve a process goal. It is, in essence, an identified risk. By providing a CSF with one or more performance indicators, it is possible to manage the risk.
Domain	A domain is the sum of policy, organization, processes, information, systems, et cetera, which we want to control as a unit and assign to a result-accountable domain owner [Klinkenberg 2002].
Function	A function is a description of a task field in which, or combination of activities to which a person is employed and primarily consists of a list of tasks to be performed within the function. A function is sometimes referred to as a profession [Coul 2001].
Functional management	Functional management is responsible for maintaining the functionality of the information system [Looijen 2004].
Functional goal	A functional goal of a service management process defines the process area of the process in terms of ICT products and ICT services.
Generic acceptance criteria	See acceptance criteria
ICT policy	ICT policy describes a more or less deliberate effort to achieve certain (business) purposes with certain (ICT) resources in a given time order (ICT policy plan) [Hoogerwerf 1972]. ICT policy must be attuned with the information policy.
ICT policy plan	An ICT policy plan is a plan that encompasses all activities (spearheads) in the time needed to implement ICT policy. The ICT policy plan includes, for example, innovation projects, renovation projects, improvement projects and maturity projects. The ICT policy plan should be attuned to the information plan.

Term	Explanation
Information policy	The information policy is derived from the corporate policy and delivers statements about how to deal with company data, information systems, ICT, the information society work organization and the use of resources for the provision of information. Finally, this policy also delivers statements about the preconditions for realizing the information policy, such as the system development and infrastructure development [Boterenbrood 2005].
Information plan	The information plan describes the migration path from the old to the new information provision.
Information provisioning architecture	An information provisioning architecture: • Is a coherent view of the information provision in the interity of the organization and its environment; • consists of descriptions of current and future establishments; • has a migration path; • has been achieved through a process of negotiation and image formation by all stakeholders; • aims to secure the interests of the organization; • thus fulfils the pivotal function between objectives of the organization and establisment of the information provision [Boterenbrood 2005].
Infrastructure as a Service (IaaS)	In this layer, the infrastructure is offered through a virtualization or hardware integration. In this layer you will find the servers, networks, storage capacity and other infrastructure. This allows the user complete freedom to the hardware. The cloud server can therefore be operated from an external location by multiple persons [Wiki].
Quality goal	The quality goal of a service management process defines the performance that the process needs to deliver.
Logical Configuration Items (LCI)	An LCI is an abstract definition of one or more related configuration items. The purpose of LCIs is to share CI information across more management domains without having to exchange all detail information. For example, based on only the most important CI attributes such as CI number, CI name, CI type, incidents, problems and change requests can be made specific and shared unambiguously across more management domains. The intention is that all management domains share each other's LCIs and administered in a Logical CMDB (LCMDB).
Maturity	The maturity of a service organization indicates the extent to which service management processes are organized to achieve the goal of the service organization. An ad hoc and task-based service organization has the lowest level. A top-level service organization has fully designed, tailored, managed, and integrated the functionality of all required service management processes to the service organization external interfaces so that they can respond permanently to the needs of the customer.
Maturity goal	The maturity objective of a service management process defines the level of maturiy that the service management process must meet. The maturity level is defined by a process maturity model, where a number of criteria that have to be met are defined per maturity level.
Maturity model	A maturity model defines the stages in which a (service) organization develops. For each stage, the requirements are described that the (service) organization has to comply with.

Term	Explanation	
Means	A means is a means of support or a means of production. In this book, a means is also called an ICT product.	
Monitoring	A service can be measured in different ways. For this purpose, the following types of monitor architectures have been defined in this book: • service desk monitoring; • built-in monitoring; • component based monitoring; • End User eXperience monitoring (EUX); • Real User Monitoring (RUM).	
	Service desk monitoring	The user himself is the registration tool and the monitor and service desk.
	Built-in monitoring	In the application, which forms the basis for the ICT service, measurement functionality is incorporated.
	Component based monitoring	Monitoring the ICT service based on the underlying infrastructure and application components.
	End User eXperience monitoring (EUX)	Monitoring based on user simulation.
	Real User Monitoring (RUM)	Monitoring based on the actual use of the ICT service.
Service Management	Service management is the maintenance of the information system components, equipment, software, data sets and procedures and related data processing and information provisioning processes in accordance with requirements and preconditions for the use and taking into account the characteristics of the defined information system components and with the People who are part of the information systems either use these systems. As such, the service management of information systems also contributes to the realization of business objectives [Looijen 2004].	
Service Management domain	A domain specifically designed for managing information systems. This may be an internal or external service organization or a mixture thereof. A service management domain can be subdivided into smaller management domains such as a service desk, front office or back office.	
Service Management tool	A service management tool is a tool for a functional, application or technical manager.	
Multi-tenant	Serving more clients based on one instance of the software.	
Organogram	An organogram is a graphical representation of the functions, roles and mutual relationships defined within an (ICT) organization.	
Platform as a Service (PaaS)	The PaaS layer offers a number of services on top of the infrastructure that enables SaaS cloud service provider to offer their applications in a structured and integrated manner. Examples of services in this layer are access management, identity management, portal functionality and integration facilities. The customer of the PaaS services is a professional technical party that, in order to fulfil his role, must have the necessary degrees of freedom within the defined boundaries. In this system, the framework and infrastructure are managed by the service provider and the user is responsible for the application software. There are often also facilities for development.	

Term	Explanation
	This is often done with a development language or framework such as Python, .NET or Java in which you can define functionalities [Wiki].
Policy starting points	In addition to a future direction (strategic positioning), the business strategy must also specify how management wants to achieve this (policy outlets): guidelines, conditions and degrees of freedom in the development of the organization and its provision of information [Beijen 2002]. This definition also applies to the ICT policy of a service organization.
Performance-indicator	A performance indicator makes a CSF measurable. A performance indicator must be assigned to a norm and a measurement unit.
Process audit	A process audit is the assessment of the design (standardization), existence and operation of a process, based on a predetermined goal (maturity, functional purpose and quality goal), independent and independent of the process. This audit is conducted by a process auditor appointed for this purpose. The following questions are asked and standards are reviewed: • What is the need for the process in the organization? • Is the process equipment and process execution in accordance with the organization's need? • Is the delivered process report on the process goals correct, complete, timely and accurate? • Are the applicable architecture principles and architectural models applied correctly? Has the service management requirements been met? • In addition, the process audit checks whether the process review has taken place.
Process implementation	A process implementation involves the design of the defined service management process in terms of methods, resources and people.
Process design	A process design is a description of the operation of a process in terms of: • process flow: processing (procedures) of input (range, information, resources), to output (resources, status, reporting); • Interaction with the environment: communication lines with business domain (s), service management domain (s) and other processes; • control: process owner, process manager, process provider, communication lines and tasks, responsibilities and competences; • Necessary people and resources: tools, Full Time Equivalent (FTE), competence profiles et cetera.
Process review	A process review evaluates the substantive functioning of the process. The review can be as well a part of the process process (e.g., the review of an RFC process) as a periodic review of the process. The following questions are asked and standards are reviewed: • Have all procedures been followed? • Have the procedures been performed correctly? • Has the work been delivered on time? • Have any errors occurred? • Have any complaints been received? • What are the reasons for not reaching the SLA norms? • What are the solutions to realize them?
Process blueprint	A process blueprint is a graphical representation depicting all managed management processes of a management organization.

Term	Explanation
	Only the main relationships between the processes are recognized. The picture is often divided into layers such as the strategic, tactical and operational layer.
Production means	The means of production concern the application software, system software, hardware and communication tools used to support an information system.
Third generation outsourcing	The third generation of outsourcing is characterized by outsourcing of ICT services to several service management parties. In addition, the management of the necessary supplier contracts can be outsourced. As a result, the client has the freedom to be serviced by various (changing) suppliers, while the management of all those parties is covered by an external supplier, the director.
Reference architecture	Reference architecture is the collection of architecture principles and architecture models. This is not limited to service management under architecture, but includes the principles and models of both business architecture, information architecture, and technical architecture, complemented by service management, security, quality assurance and legal aspects.
Role	A role is generally a position of an employee within an operations organization [Coul 2001].
Service delivery set	In ITIL version 2, this is a set of five ITIL processes that describe tactical service management: • service level management; • availability management; • capacity management; • IT Service continuity management; • financial management for IT services.
ServiceLevel Agreement (SLA)	An agreement between a customer and the ICT service provider about the deliverance of ICT services and ICT products to deliver in terms of quantity, quality and cost.
Service level management	The process of managing ICT service delivery, in terms of quality, quantity and cost, taking into account constantly changing business process needs supported by changing technologies.
Service architectuur	Creating and monitoring directional (legislative) frameworks in the form of architectural principles and architecture models (reference architecture), to achieve a consistent, future-proof and business-friendly organization of the management organization in terms of methods, resources and people through To match the IV architecture and ICT policy derived from business policy. This directionality is not limited to the designing of the service organization but also relates to the manageability of ICT products and ICT services provided by projects within the framework of the established IV architecture and managed by the management organization. In addition, the used frames used (reference architecture) are determined in meeting with the service architects with the IV architects.
Service support set	In ITIL version 2, this is a set of five ITIL processes that describe operational management, namely: • incident management;

Term	Explanation	
	• problem management; • change management; • release management; • configuration management. This set of processes includes the service desk as well.	
SMART	Specific	A concrete and clear goal with described results.
	Measurable	The desired results are measurable in terms of, for example, time, cost and / or other quantitative criteria.
	Achievable	The goal is acceptable and achievable in both the eyes of the one who determines the goal as the one who has to achieve the goal. The 'A' also stands for 'Accountable', someone has to be responsible for the intended purpose.
	Relevant	The goal is relevant and realistic given the environment / circumstances within which the goal is to be achieved.
	Time-bound	The goal is to measure progress towards the goal in terms of milestones and time.
Service management requirement	A service management requirement is a requirement regarding the functionality, quality or manageability of an ICT product and / or ICT services set by the service organization in order to ensure the objectives of the service management processes. In addition, there are service management requirements that impose requirements on the products that result from the service organisation such as process designs, procedures and resources.	
Software as a Service (SaaS)	At SaaS, the cloud service provider offers application software "through the cloud". These software can be of any kind, such as email, customer management, personnel management, video applications, et cetera. The service provider has complete control over the software, but the customer or a third party who manages the customer can in many cases configure and manage the application. In many cases, the SaaS applications can be used via a web browser on a computer. Usually, it uses modern technologies such as Ajax and HTML5 to get interactive functionality that is comparable or better than traditional client software. Many SaaS applications also work with mobile devices like smartphones and tablet computers. Also, sometimes a specific piece of client software is required and / or is the application available through a technical interface (API) [Wiki].	
Specific acceptance criteria	See acceptance criteria.	
Swimminglane	Ideally, a service management process is designed on one A4. A swim minglane is an increasingly used drawing technique for this purpose. This schematic technique consists of a number of horizontal layers. Each layer represents an actor in the service management process. By recording the procedures performed by the actor as rectangles per sheet, a blueprint decomposition (process-to-process-level) formulated. It is also possible to specify the blueprint communication lines (process level) at the procedural level.	
Task	A task is part of a task cluster that can be performed separately.	

Term	Explanation
Task cluster	A task cluster is a collection of logically coherent activities that lead to one particular result and which is generally performed by one person, as a coherent set of activities. Most of the tasks of a task cluster are homogeneous as regards the level of knowledge and / or skills required for implementation [Coul 2001].
Technical management	Technical management is responsible for maintaining the operationalization of the information system, consisting of equipment, software and data collections that must be continuously available from the use [Looijen 2014].

Appendix C, Abbreviations

This appendix lists the general abbreviations. In Appendix F, the ITIL has specific abbreviations.

Abbreviation	Meaning
ACID	Atomicity, Consistency, Isolation, Durability
API	Application Programming Interface
APM	Application Production Manual
ASL	Application Services Library
BiSL	Business information Services Library
BPaaS	Business Process as a Service
BSC	Balanced ScoreCard
BTG	Branchevereniging Telecommunicatie Grootgebruikers
CERT	Computer Emergency Readiness Team
CMMI	Capability Maturity Model Integration
CMS	Content Management System
COTS	Common Of The Shelf
CPU	Central Processing Unit
CRM	Customer Relationship Management
CRUD	Create Read Update Delete
CSB	Cloud Service Broker
CFS	Critical Success Factor
DAP	Document Agreement and Procedures
DDOS	Distributed Denial-Of-Service
DFA	Document Financial Agreements
DMZ	Demilitarized Zone
DOS	Denial Of Service
DRP	Disaster Recovery Plan
DSS	Data Security Standard
DTAP	Development-, Test-, Acceptance- and Production environment
DTS	Department of Technology Services
E2E	End-To-End
ESS	External Spec Sheet
ETL	Extract Transform Load
EUX	End User eXperience
FAQ	Frequently Asked Questions
FAT	Functional Acceptance Test
FISAA	Foreign Intelligence and Surveillance Amendments Act
FTE	Full Time Equivalent
GSA	Generic & Specific Acceptance criteria
HTML	Hyper Text Markup Language
IaaS	Infrastructure as a Service

Abbreviation	Meaning
ICT	Information & Communication Technology
IPM	Infrastructure Production Manual
ISAE	International Standard on Assurance Engagements
ISO	International Standardisation Organisation
ISS	Internal Spec Sheet
IT	Information Technology
LAN	Local Area Network
LCI	Logical Configuration Item
NIC	Network Interface Card
NPA	Network Protocol Analyse
OAT	Operational Acceptance Test
OMG	Object Management Group
PaaS	Platform as a Service
PAT	Production Acceptance Test
PCI	Payment Card Industry
PI	Performance Indicator
PoR	Programme of Requirements
PST	Performance Stress Test
QoS	Quality of Service
R&D	Research & Development
RASCI	Responsible, Accountable, Supportive, Consulted, Informed
RPC	Remote Procedure Call
RPO	Restore Point Objective
RTO	Restore Time Objective
RUM	Real User Monitoring
SaaS	Software as a Service
SABSA	Sherwoord Applied Business Security Architecture
SAML	Security Assertion Mark-up Language
SAN	Storage Area Network
SAT	Service Acceptance Test
SBB	System Building Block
SLR	Service Level Requirement
SNMP	Simple Network Management Protocol
SOX	Sarbanes OXley
SSH	Secure SHell
SSL	Secure Sockets Layer
SSO	Single Sign On
TCO	Total Cost of Ownership
TMAP Next	Test Management APproach Next
TPA	Third Party Audit
TPM	Third Party Memorandum

Abbreviation	Meaning
UAT	User Acceptance Test
URL	Uniform Resource Locator
VAT	Value Added Taxes
VLAN	Virtual Local Area Network
VOIP	Voice Over IP
VRS	Voice Response System
WAN	Wide Area Network

Appendix D, ITIL Terms

Term	Meaning
Asset management	An accounting approach for monitoring depreciation on production assets with a purchase value exceeding a predetermined threshold, by storing data on purchase value, depreciation, business unit and location.
Availability	Availability is available at any time within the agreed period. This requires continuity of information processing. High availability means that the customer can have almost continuous service because there is only a slight drop and a quick recovery.
Availability management	The purpose of availability management is to provide a cost-effective and determined level of availability of service that enables the business to achieve its goals.
Audit	A process audit is a formal review of a process to determine whether the process goals have been met and the process still fits with the needs of the user organization and management organization.
Budgeting	Budgeting concerns the activities of predicting costs and controlling expenses.
Business Continuity Management (BCM)	Business continuity management is the process of disaster management and risk management with the aim of achieving business continuity.
Business Impact Analyse (BIA)	Establishing the company's motivation to include IT Service Continuity Management in Business Continuity Management and analysing how much and what the organization has to lose in the event of a serious interruption of service provision.
Capability	Capability is the ability of an organization, person, process, application, Configuration Item (CI) or ICT service to perform an activity. It's an organization's intangible assets.
Capacity DataBase (CDB)	Building and filling the CDB is an activity that consists of collecting and maintaining technical data, business data and all other data that are important for capacity management.
Capacity management	Capacity management has the task of providing the right capacity for ICT resources continuously and in a timely manner at a reasonable cost and appropriate to the current and future needs of the customer.
Capacity management of means	The purpose of this sub process is to determine and understand the use of the ICT infrastructure.
Capacity planning	The preparation of a capacity plan analysing the existing situation (if possible by reference to scenarios) predicts the future use and resources needed to meet the expected demand for services.
Category	The term "category" is used in different management processes. Examples are an incident category, problem category and change category.

Term	Meaning
	Incident Category: An incident is subdivided into a category and subcategory, for example, based on the origin of the incident or the required dissolution group. Problem Category: Assignment to relevant domain, such as hardware, software and so on. Change Category: This is determined based on the impact and resources.
CCTA Risk Analysis and Management Method (CRAMM)	A structured method of risk analysis, resulting in a balanced mix of security measures.
Central service desk	Single contact point for all users, possibly with a separate business support desk for business applications close to users.
Change	A change is a default change or an RFC. Standard change: fully defined and approved change that needs to be registered each time but no longer has to be reviewed by change management. These are changes that can be routinely executed and can be requested at the service desk as a "call". RFC: All other requests for adjustment of the managed infrastructure.
Change Advisory Board (CAB)	This is a consultative body that is regularly convened to review and plan changes.
Change calendar	Change management is set up by change management in a change calendar or Forward Schedule of Changes (FSC). The FSC contains details of all approved changes and their planning.
Change management	Ensure that standardized methods and procedures are used so that changes can be settled in accordance with agreements.
Change request	A formal request to make a change to one or more specified CIs.
Charging	Charging involves the activities that are necessary to charge a customer for the services that delivered to him. Charging also involves determining the targets of charging as well as determining the algorithms to determine costs.
Classification	The term "classification" is used in different management processes. Examples are incident classification, problem classification and change classification. Incident Classification: The incident is given a coding of type, status, impact, urgency, priority, SLA et cetera. Incident classification aims to classify an incident so that it is better monitored and better reporting possible. Problem classification: Based on the classification, allocation of people and resources takes place and hours are available for solving a problem. The classification includes category, impact, urgency, priority and status.

Term	Meaning
	Change Classification: The classification of a change includes determining the category, urgency and priority. The category determines who is mandated to handle the change (minor change = change manager, medium change = CAB and major change = MT). The urgency determines whether the change is an urgent change or not. An urgent change will take place via the Change Advisory Board / Emergency Committee (CAB / EC). The priority indicates the order in which changes are handled.
Cold start	This option is useful for companies that can be out of service for a long time (for example 72 hours) and provide a computer at a pre-arranged location (fixed location) or portable location mobile space.
CMDB audit	With the help of audits, it can then be checked whether the current situation still matches data in the CMDB.
CMDB level of detail	This determines how much information should be available on CIs. For detailing, a plan is made for the relationships between CIs, desired CMDB draft, name and attributes (attributes) to be maintained.
Component Failure Impact Analysis (CFIA)	This method is based on an availability matrix in which service is tracked which parts of strategic importance and what role they play.
Configuration Item (CI)	Any product or service whose existence and version are registered is a CI.
Configuration management	Identify, register, verify and provide accurate information and documentation about the components of IT infrastructure to support all other service management processes.
Configuration Management Data Base (CMDB)	The CMDB can be seen as a large card box in which all IT production resources are recorded, and also all different relationships between the cards are managed.
Confidentiality	Protecting information against unauthorized knowledge and use.
Core service	A core service represents the value one or more customers want and what they want to pay for. These core services together form the actual added value for a customer.
Cost plus	The cost-plus price calculation implies that the price of a product or service is based on actual costs plus a percentage of profit. This calculation has several models that all count on the settlement of the costs incurred plus a profit margin.
Customer assets	The customer assets are a resource or capability. ITIL 2011 recognizes nine categories of customer assets to know management, organization, process, knowledge, people, information, applications, infrastructure and financial assets.
Customer outcome	The customer outcome is the result of long-term business processes. The outcome is not equal to the output of a process because the outcome is the desired end result and the output is the direct (short-term) result.
Definitive Hardware Store (DHS)	Spare parts and hardware configurations are stored in the Definitive Hardware Store. These are basic configurations that are used for replacing or repairing similar configurations in the ICT infrastructure. These are not general inventories that are stored in a warehouse.

Term	Meaning
Definitive Software Library (DSL)	Each authorized software item is physically stored in a program library called the Definitive Software Library (DSL), including all original versions of software items in operation.
Demand management	Influencing the demand for adequate ICT-components and the workload of these ICT-components.
Disaster	An event that distorts a service or system in such a way that significant measures must be taken to restore the original level of work.
Distributed Service desk	These are service desks arranged in different locations, for example in different buildings or even in different countries.
Enabling service	An enabling service enables a core service and is therefore boundary.
Enhancing service	The enhancing services are intended as an extension to the core service to make it more attractive either to reduce service more often or because of improved competitiveness.
Emergency release	An emergency issue relates to an emergency solution or a Quick Fix.
Error control	The monitoring of known errors and proposals will change.
Escalation	If an incident in the first line cannot be resolved within the agreed time, more expertise or competence must be enabled.
Evaluation	Determine if the change was a success and determine the lessons learned for the next time.
Event	A status change of a service or product that is important for service management. An event is also called alerting or notifying by a service, product or monitor tool [Cabinet Office 2011 SO].
Expert service desk	This service desk has specialist knowledge of the entire service, applications and ICT infrastructure and the expertise to solve most incidents and problems themselves. In practice, the norm of 80% solving power is often set to the expert service desk.
External underpinning contract	An external underlying contract is a contract with an external supplier in which agreements regarding the care of certain parts of a service are recorded.
Fault Time	The time between the occurrence of a malfunction and the restoration of service.
Fault Tree Analysis (FTA)	FTA is a technique used to determine the chain of events that could lead to a malfunction of a service.
Financial Management for IT services	Financial management for IT services is an integral part of service management. It provides essential management information needed to ensure efficient and cost-effective service provision. An efficient financial management system enables the ICT organization to fully account for expenses and to pay it to the services provided to the customer.
First line support	The first line is usually the service desk.
Forward Schedule of Changes (FSC)	See change calendar.
Full release	Full release means that the entire program is redistributed, including those that have not been changed.

Term	Meaning
Functional escalation	Functional escalation involves the inclusion of more specialization or access rights (technical competence) in the dissolution process, with sometimes division boundaries being exceeded. This is also referred to as routing.
Going rate	The going rate concerns standard price agreements for services.
Help desk	Because the traditional Help desk gets an ever-wider task, it is now referred to as service desk.
Hierarchical escalation	This makes use of higher layers of the organization because the current authority is insufficient (organizational competence, power) or the resources for solving are not sufficiently available.
Hot start	This option concerns an immediate or very fast recovery (less than 24 hours) of service through a duplicate production environment and data reflection or self-processing.
Identification	Identification focuses on determining and maintaining naming and version numbering of the physical components of the ICT infrastructure, the underlying relationships and the relevant attributes.
Impact	The impact of an incident is the level of deviation from the normal service level, in numbers of users or business processes that are affected.
Incident	An incident is an event that does not belong to the standard operation of a service and which causes or may cause an interruption or a reduction in the quality of that service.
Incident management	Incident management has the reactive task of eliminating the effects of (imminent) malfunctioning in services and ensuring that users can get back to work as quickly as possible.
Information security management	The purpose of information security management is twofold.
Interruption	See malfunction.
Known Error	A known error is a problem whose cause has been successfully identified.
Lead time	Lead time of a change is the time elapsing from the submission of an RFC to the realization of the change in the production environment.
Line Of Service (LOS)	A LOS is a core service or service package that includes more service options. A LOS is managed by a service owner. Each service option is intended to operate a particular market segment.
Malfunction	An event that eliminates the agreed service (threatened).
Mean Time Between Failure (MTBF)	The average time between the recovery of one incident and the occurrence of the next incident, also called uptime.
Mean Time To Repair (MTTR)	The average time between occurrence of a malfunction and the reset of the service, also known as downtime.
Message	Every time a user calls the service desk there is a call. There are two main categories of calls to know incidents and changes.
Modelling	Modelling is part of the capacity management process and is used to predict the behaviour of the infrastructure.
Negotiated Contract Price	A negotiated contract price is a price for an ICT product or ICT service negotiated with the customer.

Term	Meaning
	The sub-deal with the customer includes, for example, whether the customer has to pay all investment costs or only part of it.
Notional charging	This implies that a pro forma settlement of costs takes place. The costs are billed, but have not yet been paid.
Maintenance	Corrective maintenance: Activities caused by software imperfections not noted by test environments. Preventive maintenance: Improvements offered by vendors based on errors that have not yet produced production problems but may possibly be possible. Perfective maintenance: Improve the performance level of the software, which will provide more functionality. Adaptive maintenance: Software modifications for external causes, such as hardware change, merger of companies And become obsolete with software. Additive maintenance: Extending the software for interfaces with the outside world.
Maintenance ability	Maintenance ability concerns the effort required to keep a service operational, or to restore this service if it fails. This includes preventive maintenance: and periodic inspections.
Malfunction	An event that eliminates the agreed service (threatened).
Mutual Agreement	This option is used when two organizations have similar machines and decide to deliver each other in emergency capacity.
Opening time	The time that a service (e.g., the service desk) is provided (available or available).
Operation	Operation includes all the day-to-day infrastructure management tasks of the computing centre that are required to secure the agreed management service to the customer, such as backup / restore, monitoring, batch processing, stopping and staring of services, event management, deployment and the like.
Operational Level Agreement (OLA)	An OLA is an agreement with an (internal) IT department that deals with the provision of care for certain parts of a service, such as an OLA on the availability of the network or the availability of print servers. An OLA serves to support the ICT organization providing the service.
Package release	A bundled release (package release) is a release that rolls out both a complete set of application modules of one or more associated applications (full release) as the last patches (delta). An example is the roll-out of a particular release of MS Windows plus MS Office including the latest service pack and patches.
Patterns of Business Activities (PBA)	A PBA is a workload pattern of one or more business activities. PBAs are used to provide the service provider with insight into the various levels of business activities so that service provision can be better tailored to this.

Term	Meaning
	Examples of PBAs are: frequency of remote customer management, frequency of on-site customer visits, handling sensitive information and printing documents and images. The business activities of these patterns are defined by attributes such as frequency, duration, et cetera.
Performance management	Measurement, monitoring and tuning of the performance of the components of the ICT infrastructure.
Post Implementation Review (PIR)	A PIR is an evaluation after implementation. Before the problem can be completed, the change must first be evaluated. A PIR is held for this purpose. In doing so, attention is paid to: • Has the change reached its intended purpose? • Are users satisfied with the result? • Have there been any side effects? • Are the estimated costs and efforts not exceeded?
Price policy	The pricing policy because the choices that determine the price of a product or service. Within ITIL, there are a number of possibilities for this: • cost plus; • going rate; • negotiated contract price; • notional charging; • what the market will bear.
Priority	Of an incident: The priority is a number based on urgency (how fast should it be restored) and on impact (how serious is the disturbance). Of a problem: Combination of urgency, impact, risk and resources needed. Of a change: Indicates the importance of the change and is a derivative of urgency and impact.
Proactive problem Management	To prevent incidents due to errors in the infrastructure.
Problem	A problem describes an unwanted situation indicating the still unknown cause of one or more existing or potential incidents.
Problem control	Define and investigate problems.
Problem management	Problem management investigates the infrastructure and available registrations, including the incident database, to identify causes for (potential) malfunctions in service.
Procedure	A procedure is a description of a logically coherent series of activities, stating the executives. A procedure can contain phases of different processes.
Process	A process is a logically coherent series of activities that are performed to realize a predetermined goal.
Process manager	It is the task of the process manager to ensure that the process is carried out efficiently and effectively through planning and control.
Software item	Each authorized software item is (physically) stored in the DSL, including all original versions of software items in operation.

Term	Meaning
Provisioning	Provisioning is the automatic creation, modification or removal of identity data in other systems in order to reduce management costs.
Quality control	Organizing, introducing and monitoring quality assurance.
Quality assurance	The whole of measures and procedures that ensure the organization ensures that the service continues to meet customer expectations and the agreements made with the customer.
Registration	The registration includes capturing information about a call, incident, problem, change, configuration item or change.
Registering service desk	On a registering service desk, calls are registered and quickly routed. The staffing consists of non-IT technically skilled staff with communicative skills.
Repair	The restoration of the agreed service is the phase in which the service is brought back to air after a disruption and released to the user organization.
Repairability	The ability to recover from a disturbance, this may be functional, technical, or in time.
Resolving service desk	This service desk has more knowledge and expertise than call centre and unskilled service desk, can solve many incidents based on documented solutions, but also routing a part to solving groups. The staffing consists of, to a degree, ICT-technically-educated staff, who also has communicative skills.
Relation	Relation of a CI.
Release	A release version is composed of one or more changes. A rollout (release) concerns the distribution of a product or service. A release can be rolled out in several ways: • full release; • package release; • release.
Release management	Release management performs the management and distribution of software hardware versions that are in use and are supported by the ICT department. In order to meet the required level of service.
Release plan	A release plan describes how, what, what, where and when is distributed.
Release policy	The release manager sets up a release policy in advance, which determines how and when releases are compiled.
Release unit	The unit of an edition that is usually rolled out at the same time.
Reliability	A sufficient degree of reliability means that the service remains available for a fixed period of time.
Resilience	The ability of a service or component to function properly despite the inoperative functioning of one or more subsystems (resistance to failure).
Resource	Resource is a common term for resources, including ICT infrastructure, people, capital or other things that help to provide the ICT service. Resources are considered as (tangible) assets of an organization.
Review	Each process is reviewed periodically. This ensures that all procedures are performed correctly. A review can be performed within the process, such as the review of an incident, problem or change. In that case, the review is a process within the process. In addition, a review can be carried out separately from the process.

Term	Meaning
	This process review can be formalized with norms or informal without a standard framework.
Risk	A risk is a possible undesired event with certain negative consequences. To determine the risk of a product, the vulnerabilities and threats are deposited against the means of production. This follows an assessment of the risks.
Security	Safety is to be safe from known risks and to minimize unconscious risks. Security is the means to this end. Information security management is the process that takes care of this.
Security section	The starting point when setting up the security clause in the SLA is the security needs of the customer. The SLA's security section may include issues such as the general security policy, a list of authorized persons, procedures for protecting property, restrictions on copying information, and so forth.
Security incident	A security incident is an incident where the event violates the security policy of the affected system.
Security levels	Service level management distinguishes a number of coherent security activities in which information security management plays an important role, such as proposing, negotiating and capturing the desired level of security of the SLA services. When determining the SLA, it is generally assumed that there is a general level of security (basic security level, or security baseline).
Serviceability	Maintenance level refers to the contractual maintenance obligation of external service providers. Contract has been invested in the support of external services.
Service	A service is a way to deliver added value to the customer by helping a customer achieve the desired end results, without being liable for the specific costs or risks.
Service asset	Any resource or capability of a service provider. The service assets include everything that can contribute to providing a customer service to the customer. Within ITIL 2011, the following classes of service assets are recognized: management, organization, processes, knowledge, capital, infrastructure, applications, information and people.
Service catalogue	Creating a service catalogue is an excellent way for the ICT organization to profile itself. The service catalogue provides a detailed overview of the (operational) services and the associated service levels that the ICT organization can offer to its clients, and is therefore an important means of communication.
Service desk	The service desk aims to support the agreed service by ensuring the accessibility and accessibility of the ICT organization and by carrying out a number of supportive activities.
Service Improvement Programme (SIP)	In the SIP, the implementation of which is often formally implemented in the form of a project, actions, phases and performance data are documented that aim to improve service.
Service Level Agreement (SLA)	A service level agreement is an agreement that has been defined by the ICT organization and customer agreements about the services to be delivered.

Term	Meaning
Service level management	Service level management is the process of negotiating, defining, measuring, controlling and improving the quality of service at fair costs.
Service level requirements	Service level requirements consist of a detailed record of customer needs and are used to set up, modify and renew services.
Service levels	In order to allow the customer to choose a certain price / performance ratio, different levels of services (service levels) are often defined. Often service levels are defined in terms of metals such as gold, silver and bronze.
Service management	The goal of the processes of IT service management is ultimately to contribute to the quality of service provision.
Service norm	In order to be able to monitor SLAs, service norms must be well defined in advance and agreed with the externally agreed target values.
Service option	If service packages have to be offered to different types of customers in different ways, one or more components of the service package can be modified. Also, the functionality (utility) and quality (warranty) can be divided over a number of levels, called service options. Service packages and service options are designed in terms of functionality and quality to meet the requirements of specific PBAs.
Service package	A service package is a collection of two or more core services, enabling services or enhancing services that are offered to customers to provide a solution for a spicy type of customer support to achieve a specific operating result. A service package may also include one or more service packages.
Service provisioning	Service provisioning is the total management (maintenance and operation) or the ICT infrastructure.
Service request	The ITIL definition of incidents does not only include hardware and software disruptions, but also service requests. This is a request from the user for support, delivery, information, advice or documentation.
Status	The status of an incident, problem, change or release indicates which stage of the life cycle it is.
Status incident	It is the duty of the service desk to inform the user about the status of his incidents.
System Outage Analysis (SOA)	SOA is a technique that can be used to find out the causes of malfunctions, to investigate the effectiveness of ICT organization and processes, and to present and implement improved proposals.
Second line support	The support in the 2nd line by the management departments.
Third line support	The assistance in solving incidents or problems offered by professional specialists (developers, administrators and architects) after the support of the second line did not result in a timely outcome.
Tuning	Tuning is the optimal setting of systems at actual or expected workload based on measured, analysed and interpreted data.
User	The user of a service.
Urgent change	Despite all the plans, it may still happen that a change should take immediate priority. Urgent changes are characterized by the great and urgent importance associated with their execution.

Term	Meaning
	In most cases, immediate resources for other activities must be released immediately.
Urgency	Of an incident: The amount of postponement that can tolerate the user or the business process. Of a problem: The extent to which postponement of solution accepts table. Of a change: The urgency of a change determines whether or not a change is classified as an urgent change.
User profile	A defined pattern of user demand for ICT services. Each user profile includes one or more PBAs.
Verification	In addition to the formal audits initiated from configuration management, the service desk can verify certain items from the CMDB directly in contact with the customer when receiving an incident report.
Version	A version is a new edition of software with one or more adjustments. Modifications to software can be large, small and marginal. A major customization of software is usually rolled out in the form of a release. For minor adjustments, a version is used and a patch for marginal adjustments.
Version number	A version number is a unique identifier of software customization. Often software is assigned an identification number with the following composition: release number.version number.patch number.
Virtual service desk	A service desk that consists of a number of local service desks that together form a seemingly whole. It does not matter where the service desk and the support are located.
Vulnerability	The degree of sensitivity to malfunctions due to insufficient management and / or security measures.
Warm Stand-by	This option concerns access to a similar operational environment where, after a short switching time (24-72 hours), the services can simply turn on.
What the market will bear	What the market will bear is a term that indicates that the prices used are in proportion to the prices that the market uses.
Workaround	After classification, it is checked whether a similar incident occurred and whether there is a solution or a temporary solution (workaround). Problem management supports incident management by providing workarounds and quick fixes. Problem management ensures that symptoms and malfunctions are documented.
Work instruction	A work instruction explains one or more activities in a procedure to determine how they should be performed.
Workload	One of the results of capacity management consists of workload characteristics. These can be used to predict what the required capacity will be, for example, the number of users grows by 25%. Capacity management includes application sizing. This part of capacity management determines the hardware or network capacity needed to support new (or customized) applications, including the workload.

Appendix E, ITIL Abbreviations

Abbreviation	Meaning
BCM	Business Continuity Management
BIA	Business Impact Analysis
BSI	British Standards Institute
CAB	Change Advisory Board
CAB / EC	Change Advisory Board / Emergency Committee
CCTA	Central Computer Telecommunications Agency
CDB	Capacity Management Database
CFIA	Component Failure Impact Analysis
CI	Configuration Item
CIA	Confidentiality Integrity Accessibility
CMDB	Configuration Management DataBase
CRAMM	CCTA's Risk Analysis Management Methodology
CRUD	Create Read Update Delete
CSF	Critical Success Factor
CSI	Continual Service Improvement
DHS	Definitive Hardware Store
DSL	Definitive Software Library
FSC	Forward Schedule of Changes
FTA	Fault Tree Analysis
IT	Information Technology
ITIL	Information Technology Infrastructure Library
ITSCM	Infrastructure Technology Service Continuity Management
KPI	Key Performance Indicator
LOS	Lines of Service
MTBF	Mean Time Between Failures
MTBSI	Mean Time Between System Incidents
MTTR	Mean Time To repair
OLA	Operational Level Agreement
PBA	Patterns of Business Activity
PDCA	Plan Do Check Act
PEN test	Penetration test
PIR	Post Implementation Review
PSA	Projected Service Availability
RACI	Responsible, Accountable, Supportive, Consulted, Informed
RFC	Request For Change
RFP	Request for Proposal
RPC	Remote Procedure Call
SIP	Service Improvement Programme (Service Improvement Plan)

Abbreviation	Meaning
SLA	Service Level Agreement
SMART	Specific, Measurable, Achievable, Relevant and Time-boud.
SOA	System Outage Analysis
SPOC	Single Point Of Contact
SPOF	Single Point Of Failure
SQP	Service Quality Plan
TOP	Technical Observation Post
UC	Underpinning Contract

Appendix F, Websites

Balanced scorecard	[BSC]	http://www.balanced_scorecard.nl / indexsu.htm
BTG	[BTG 2012]	http://btg.org / 2012 / 10 / 13 / debat-over-cloudcomputing-wordt-vertroebeld-door-onbegrip-over-patriot-act /
Computable	[Computable]	http://www.computable.nl / Article / opinie / cloud_computing / 4635150 / 2333364 / patriot-act-het-wordt-nog-erger.html#ixzz2NuMxYTKk
Datamotion	[Datamotion]	http://www.datamation.com /
Dbmetrics	[dbmetrics]	http://www.dbmetrics.nl
De ITSMF page	[ITSMF]	http://www.itsmf.nl
Deming	[Deming]	http://www.pathmaker.com / resources / leaders / ishikawa.htm
EXIN	[Exin]	http://www.exin.nl
FCW	[FCW 2013]	http://www.fcw.com / articles / 2013 / 01 / 07 / cloud-broker.aspx
Forbes	[Forbes 2012]	http://www.forbes.com / sites / gartnergroup / 2012 / 03 / 22 / cloud-services-brokerage-a-must-have-for-most-organizations /
GPO	[GPO]	http://www.gpo.gov / fdsys / pkg / PLAW-107publ56 / html / PLAW-107publ56.htm
IIR	[IIR]	http://www.IIR.nl
ITMG	[ITMG]	http://www.ITMG.nl
Information management	[INFO]	http://www.information-management.com/news/cloud_data_security_storage_GRC_virtualization_EU-10019518-1.html
ITIL	[ITIL]	http://www.ITIL.nl
ITIL opleidingen	[Opleidingen]	http://www.ITMG.nl
Kwintes	[Kwintes]	http://www.kwintes.nl
NGI	[NGI]	http://www.ngi.nl
NIST	[NIST]	http://csrc.nist.gov / publications / nistpubs / 800-145 / SP800-145.pdf
Cabinet Office	[Cabinet Office]	http://www.cabinetoffice.gov.uk /
Trouw	[Trouw 2011]	http://www.trouw.nl / tr / nl / 5133 / Media-technologie / article / detail / 3065081 / 2011 / 12 / 05 / Patriot-Act-keert-zich-tegen-Amerikaanse-technologiesector.dhtml
Wiki	[Wiki]	http://nl.wikipedia.org / wiki / Cloud_computing
ZDNET	[ZDNET]	http://www.zdnet.com / blog / igeneration / google-admits-patriot-act-requests-handed-over-european-data-to-u-s-authorities / 12191

Appendix G, Index

W

WAN · 65, 123
warm stand-by · 29
warrant · 89
warranty · 25, 26, 27, 29, 30, 32, 52, 53, 54, 89, 95, 134
warranty period · 54
watertight · 14, 53
web · 6
web application · 74
what the market will bear · 131, 135

Wide Area Network · see WAN
Wintel platform · 70
work instruction · 130
workaround · 83, 135
workflow management · 67
workload · 135
wrap license contract · 18

Z

Z/OS · 76

About the authors

Bart has been active in ICT since 1985. He worked primarily with the top 100 of Dutch business and government organizations. He has acquired experience in different roles within all aspects of system development, including operations for 12 years. After that, he focused on the subject of service management.

Currently, as a consultant, he is active in all aspects of the knowledge management cycle of service management, such as training ICT managers and service managers, advising service management organisations, improving service management processes and outsourcing (parts of) service management organisations. He graduated at both the HTS and University level in the management field.

Pascal is the Chief Technology Officer (CTO) at Fujitsu for large accounts in EMEIA where he drives digital business innovation and digital transformation. He has a background in IT strategy, Enterprise Architecture and Innovation and worked for many governments, inter-organizational projects, insurance companies and banks. Pascal has a Master in Business Administration, a bachelor in Information Technology and he joined a management program on Oxford University/Said business school). He is an actionable digital-native who focusses on maximizing his impact to deliver practical results. Besides his strategic business focus and his knowledge of multiple business domains like marketing, online and entrepreneurship he has a very strong background in IT with in-depth knowledge of many IT topics. Pascal is the Former CTO of Delta Lloyd where he was responsible for driving Innovation, direction of the strategic programs, architecture and the CIO Office.

Pascal has worked for many organizations as an Enterprise Architect and management consultant, working for a consulting firm and his own firm "Strategic Consulting Alliance". Besides his corporate work he also founded two startups and he participated actively in several communities such as the Enterprise architecture, sourcing, and CxO community. Pascal is an author of several articles on IT strategy, Enterprise Architecture and Cloud and a frequent speaker on several CxO and innovation conferences and seminars.

Other books by these authors

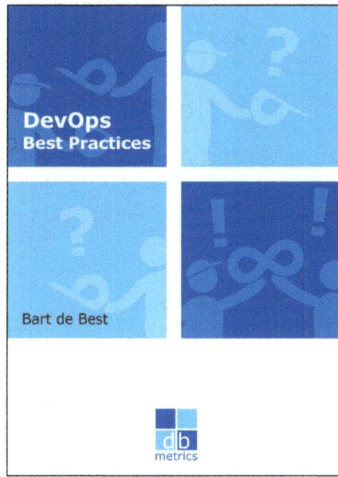

DevOps Best Practices
Best Practices for DevOps

In recent years, many organisatons have experienced the benefits of using Agile approaches such as Scrum and Kanban. The software is delivered faster whilst quality increases and costs decrease. The fact that many organisations that applied the Agile approach did not take into account the traditional service management techniques, in terms of information management, application management and instrastructure management, is a major disadvantage. The solution to this problem has been found in the Dev (Development) Ops (Operations) approach. Both worlds are merged into one team, thus sharing the knowledge and skills. This book is about sharing knowledge on how DevOps teams work together. For each aspect of the DevOps process best practices are given in 30 separate articles. For each aspect of the DevOps process best practices are given in 30 separate articles. The covered aspects are: Plan, Code, Build, Test, Release, Deploy, Operate and Monitor. Each article starts with the definition of the specifically used terms and one or more concepts. The body of each article is kept simple, short and easy to read.

Author   : Bart de Best
Publisher : Leonon Media, 2017
ISBN   : 978 94 92618 078

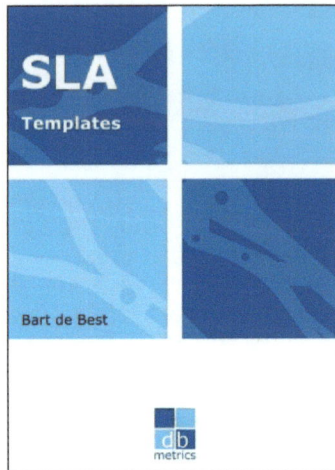

SLA Templates
A complete set of SLA templates

The most important thing in providing a service Is that the customer is satisfied with the delivered performance. With this satisfaction, the supplier gets re-purchasing's, promotions in the market and is the continuity of the company ensured. Perhaps the most important aspect of this customer satisfaction for a supplier is that the employees in question get a drive to further develop their own knowledge and skills to satisfy even more customers. This book describes the templates for Service Level Agreements in order to agree with the customer on the required service levels.

This book gives both a template and an explanation for this template for all common service level management documents.

The following templates are included in this book:
- Service Level Agreement (SLA)
- Underpinning Contract (UC)
- Operational Level Agreement (OLA)
- Document Agreement and Procedures (DAP)
- Document Financial Agreements (DFA)
- Service Catalogue
- External Spec Sheet (ESS)
- Internal Spec Sheet (ISS)
- Service Quality Plan (SQP)
- Service Improvement Program (SQP)

Author   : Bart de Best
Publisher   : Leonon Media, 2017
ISBN   : 978 94 92618 030